DEDICATION

This work is dedicated to the true love of my life, our Lord and Savior Jesus! It is also dedicated to my awesome wife, Alice Lee, whom God has called His Bride!

TABLE OF CONTENTS

PREFACE

I grew up in a traditional church. There was no call for salvation, no invitation to prayer, no encouragement to come deeper into the Lord. But, every Sunday the Pastor would say: "Let us reverently attend to this reading of God's Holy Word."

In desperation and in depression I began calling out to see if there really was a God. After months of begging Him to reveal Himself, He spoke to me audibly. He said: "I love you. I have always loved you. Now I want you to go and tell others that I love them, too." He imparted to me a great deal of information about the body of Christ, His plan, His desires for us, His call on my life, His soon return, and He required me to get water baptized.

I cried and laughed for three days; so much so that my face literally hurt. I thought I was in Heaven! I thought everything would be OK, now. I thought He was coming back immediately.

As time passed, I realized that He was not coming IMMEDIATELY. "Soon" meant something different to Him than to me. I got into the Word and read *In His Steps*, by Charles Sheldon. I began to question what I saw around me. My church experience did not reflect His Word. My life did not appear to be a "new creation" and much of the old had still not "passed away." (2 Corinthians 5:17). I missed the sense of oneness that I had experienced with Him when He first spoke to me. I WANTED MORE.

Years later, I met people who said they had more. I came to understand the infilling of God's Spirit and His spiritual gifts. Now, I thought, I will have it all. THIS is what it is all about.

Then I began to look around and realized that many who claimed to have it all, did not reflect what I saw in the Word. We spoke of power, but displayed little. We called him Lord, but did whatever pleased us. I WANTED MORE.

Church work consumed my time and my energy. I knew what the church was supposed to be and I tried my best to create

His church. But, no matter how I tried, I couldn't make it right. I looked around and didn't think too highly of Body of Christ. People in the church were ego-driven, rebellious, fractious, resentful, and exalting the flesh. I WANTED MORE.

I tried to work for the unity of the body: pastors standing with pastors, churches standing with churches, to the glory of God, One Lord, One Baptism, One Church, One Kingdom. I found rejection and doors slammed in my face. I found selfish, self-centered kingdom builders who ignored God's commandment to love one another.

I experienced the revival of the early 1970's. I saw the deaf hear, the blind see, the crippled walk, and the dead raised. I looked around and realized that even though we now had power, the lives of believers did not reflect the Word. I remembered the intimacy that I had first experienced and missed it. I WANTED MORE.

We got involved in world missions, raised a lot of money and saw souls won. I built home missions and educational ministries. It did not satisfy.

I was invited to participate in Christian television and radio. Jim Bakker and Jimmy Swaggart were my contemporaries. The more I saw, I definitely WANTED MORE FROM GOD!

We heard the call to prayer and intercession. We learned how to pray, powerfully. We sought God in the early morning and prayed fervently. I was still unsatisfied.

I read *The Practice of the Presence of God*, by Brother Lawrence. I heard about going on a "God hunt," which leads us to find God's presence in our daily lives. I WANTED MORE!

We learned to worship. We experienced deep, prophetic, anointed worship in which people were sovereignly saved, healed and delivered. I thought we were finally there. But quickly worship turned to ego, performance, and professionalism. I watched Christian music artists who said: "God gave me this worship song. It is for His glory," as they sued churches for using THEIR songs in worship without paying the copyrights. I WANTED MORE.

I sought education and professional competence. I was still unsatisfied.

I was learning to die to self throughout this quest: growing, dying, growing, dying. I STILL WANTED MORE.

Then God called me to lay it all down. To become a nobody in no place, where it would be He and I, without distractions. He removed everything I had, so that I would have to cry out to Him. There I heard Him say once again: "I love you!"

James A. Laine, Ph.D.
Phoenix, Arizona
May 2000

INTRODUCTION

"...God is love." 1 John 4:8. God is love. Love needs someone to love and someone to love back. I started looking for a wife at age eleven. I can remember crying myself to sleep, because I so wanted to be loved and to have someone to love. I made poor choices, latching onto any girl who even looked capable of affection. My heart was broken many times. I latched on too tightly and consumed all I could get. Too much, too soon, too many, too many wrong choices. It wasn't until I met my wife and God said: "this is the woman you are going to marry" that I found real love in the human arena.

I can still remember the void and the pain of feeling unloved and of not having someone to love.

God's Need

Imagine this: God is love. That is not just what He does, it is Who and what He is. From eternities past, for all eternity past, God has had no one to love and no one to love Him. He was alone, totally alone. The void! The emptiness! The desire! The need! The hunger! The loneliness!

Then, somewhere in forever, He created other beings with whom He could relate. He created angels, archangels, cherubim and seraphim. But, there was not found a real love for Him. They all lacked the ability for real love.

Adam and Eve

He showed this to us by creating Adam and showing him how it felt to not be able to find a helpmate meet for him! He demonstrated His need and His desire in Adam.

8

Free Will is Required

Real love requires freedom of choice because LOVE IS THE DESIRE TO BLESS THE OTHER PERSON AT MY EXPENSE, and LOVE IS AN ACT OF OUR FREE WILL.

All of those created beings lacked free will. So, even though God now had companions and others with whom to relate and watch over, He still lacked anyone who could give Him love.

The answer seems so easy. He is God, why didn't He just make someone who was capable of loving Him? That is what He did. He made you. But, it wasn't easy, or without a tremendous cost to Him.

The Dilemma

Here is the dilemma: Love not only requires free will to choose to love or not to love, it also requires a real alternative. In other words, love *this* or love *that*. It couldn't be simply just *love* or don't *love*. It would be like saying that you can have any car you want. However, the only brand of car that exists is Chevy. So, feel free to choose.

To create a being capable of real love required allowing a real choice. It required allowing evil to come into existence. And, allowing the existence of evil required a mechanism to deal with evil. Allowing the existence of evil would mean that sin would infect even the ones who would choose to love God. And, since God is Holy and Pure, He cannot look on sin, relate to sin, or allow sin in His presence. The idea of allowing evil and then having to clean it up, for the sake of love, is mind-boggling.

The Price of Real Love

The Blood

The price of dealing with the sin that would contaminate all of God's prospective lovers is the blood of His own Son. Jesus would have to die in our place so that we could be washed and made clean before we could enter the presence of the Lord. (Hebrews).

The Price of Real Love

The Rejection

Another reality of allowing choice is that it becomes unavoidable that God would have to suffer the rejection of those who chose not to love Him. He would have to exchange the emptiness of having no one to love Him for the pain of giving His own Son for us and having us choose to reject Him.

All He wanted was for us to love Him, but most of us have chosen not to love Him. Even when He sent Jesus to redeem us "He came unto His own and His own received Him not." John 1:11. If we are ever going to experience real love, we have to risk rejection.

For God to experience real love, He had to create us, deal with evil and sin, the Fall, the crucifixion and the rejection of those He loved. He chose to pay the price. As a result, we have the opportunity to experience the most incredible love that exists: The love between God and His Bride!

CHAPTER ONE

LOVE

One of the Pharisees asked: "Teacher, which is the great commandment in the law?" Jesus answered him: "You shall love the Lord your God with all your heart, and with all your soul, and with all your mind." Matthew 22:35-37. He quoted directly from Deuteronomy 6:5.

In fact, the primary purpose of the Word is to tell us of God's love for us and then to lead us to love God. The primary purpose for Jesus coming was to reconcile us to the Father so that we could love Him. Our response to the love of Jesus is to love Him back. "We love because He first loved us." 1 John 4:19. In fact, the entire Word is a love story replete with intense passion and the excruciating pain of rejection, loss, lust and adultery.

Love holds a unique place in the Word. As just stated, it is Old Testament law. It is *the* New Testament commandment. It is the principle of the Golden Rule. It is a gift. It is fruit. It is the nature of God. It is the reason for creation and the reason for free will. It is the reason for salvation. Nothing else fits all of these categories.

Love is also found in every kind of Bible literature. It is in the history recorded by the Word. It is in the wisdom, the poetry, the prophecy, the Gospels, and the letters. Nothing else is found in all these forms of Scripture. Let's look at it.

Love is the Great Commandment of the Law

Love is the great commandment of the law. (Matthew 22:35-37, Deuteronomy 6:5). Love is also the underlying principle behind the various Old Testament laws presented by God. Some may find this hard to believe, but it is true.

The Ten Commandments

Love is the foundation principle of the Ten Commandments found in Exodus 20:1f. All of the commandments are directed toward the love of God or the love of others. They reflect the two great commandments in Matthew 22; love God, love your neighbor.

Love was the Requirement of the Law

"12 And now, Israel, what doth the LORD thy God require of thee, but to fear the LORD thy God, to walk in all his ways, and to love him, and to serve the LORD thy God with all thy heart and with all thy soul, 13 To keep the commandments of the LORD, and his statutes, which I command thee this day for thy good? 14 Behold, the heaven and the heaven of heavens is the LORD'S thy God, the earth also, with all that therein is. 15 Only the LORD had a delight in thy fathers to love them, and he chose their seed after them, even you above all people, as it is this day. 16 Circumcise therefore the foreskin of your heart, and be no more stiffnecked. 17 For the LORD your God is God of gods, and Lord of lords, a great God, a mighty, and a terrible, which regardeth not persons, nor taketh reward: 18 He doth execute the judgment of the fatherless and widow, and loveth the stranger, in giving him food and raiment. 19 Love ye therefore the stranger: for ye were strangers in the land of Egypt. 20 Thou shalt fear the LORD thy God; him shalt thou serve, and to him shalt thou cleave, and swear by his name. 21 He is thy praise, and he is thy God, that hath done for thee these great and terrible things, which thine eyes have seen." Deuteronomy 10:12-21.

Many of God's Laws were Based on Love for Neighbors

"1 Thou shalt not see thy brother's ox or his sheep go astray, and hide thyself from them: thou shalt in any case bring them again unto thy brother. 2 And if thy brother be not nigh unto thee, or if thou know him not, then thou shalt bring it unto thine own house, and it shall be with thee until thy brother seek after it, and thou shalt restore it to him again. 3 In like manner shalt thou do with his ass; and so shalt thou do with his raiment; and with all lost thing of thy brother's, which he hath lost, and thou hast found, shalt thou do likewise: thou mayest not hide thyself. 4 Thou shalt not see thy brother's ass or his ox fall down by the way, and hide thyself from them: thou shalt surely help him to lift them up again." Deuteronomy 22:1-4.

"18 Thou shalt not avenge, nor bear any grudge against the children of thy people, but thou shalt love thy neighbour as thyself: I am the LORD. ...34 But the stranger that dwelleth with you shall be unto you as one born among you, and thou shalt love him as thyself; for ye were strangers in the land of Egypt: I am the LORD your God." Leviticus 19:18, 34.

Many of God's Laws Were Based on Love for the Ignorant

"Thou shalt not plow with an ox and an ass together." Deuteronomy 22:10. The Children of Israel were not farmers. They did not know how to farm productively. God saved them the frustration of learning that and ox and an ass will not work together; they will only frustrate the farmer.

Many of God's Laws were Based on Love for Animals

"Thou shalt not muzzle the ox when he treadeth out the corn." Deuteronomy 25:4. Animals need to be taken care of, not just used to serve us.

Many of God's Laws were Based on Love for Society

"If thou meet thine enemy's ox or his ass going astray, thou shalt surely bring it back to him again." Exodus 23:4. Common decency, love and respect for one another is required if we find an animal that belongs to another we return it, even if we do not *like* the other person.

"Whosoever lieth with a beast shall surely be put to death." Exodus 22:19.

Perversion destroys a society.

"A man also or woman that hath a familiar spirit, or that is a wizard, shall surely be put to death: they shall stone them with stones: their blood shall be upon them." Leviticus 20:27.

Occult practices, which serve Satan, destroy a society.

"And he that killeth any man shall surely be put to death." Leviticus 24:17.

God knows that sex sin, murder, occult practice, etc., pollute a society. Because of His love for us, He commands that those who do such things should be put to death.

Many of God's Laws were Based on Love for the Individual

"Six days thou shalt do thy work, and on the seventh day thou shalt rest: that thine ox and thine ass may rest, and the son of thy handmaid, and the stranger, may be refreshed." Exodus 23:12

Love is the Basis of the
Three New Testament Commandments

"37 Jesus said unto him, Thou shalt love the Lord thy God with all thy heart, and with all thy soul, and with all thy mind. 38 This is the first and great commandment. 39 And the second is like unto it, Thou shalt love thy neighbour as thyself. 40 On these two commandments hang all the law and the prophets." Matthew 22:37-40. [Love is the basis for everything given in the law and the prophets.]

"A new commandment I give unto you, That ye love one another; as I have loved you, that ye also love one another." John 13:34.

Love is a Gift

"And hope maketh not ashamed; because the love of God is shed abroad in our hearts by the Holy Ghost which is given unto us." Romans 5:5.

Love is Fruit

"22 But the fruit of the Spirit is love, joy, peace, longsuffering, gentleness, goodness, faith, 23 Meekness, temperance: against

14

such there is no law. 24 And they that are Christ's have crucified the flesh with the affections and lusts." Galatians 5:22-24.

Did you ever notice that the Word says **the fruit** of the Spirit **is** love? It does not say the fruits of the spirit *are* .... That is because all of the words that follow are characteristics of love.

Joy comes from love.

"8 Herein is my Father glorified, that ye bear much fruit; so shall ye be my disciples. 9 As the Father hath loved me, so have I loved you: continue ye in my love. 10 If ye keep my commandments, ye shall abide in my love; even as I have kept my Father's commandments, and abide in his love. 11 These things have I spoken unto you, that my joy might remain in you, and that your joy might be full. 12 This is my commandment, That ye love one another, as I have loved you. 13 Greater love hath no man than this, that a man lay down his life for his friends. 14 Ye are my friends, if ye do whatsoever I command you. 15 Henceforth I call you not servants; for the servant knoweth not what his lord doeth: but I have called you friends; for all things that I have heard of my Father I have made known unto you. 16 Ye have not chosen me, but I have chosen you, and ordained you, that ye should go and bring forth fruit, and that your fruit should remain: that whatsoever ye shall ask of the Father in my name, he may give it you. 17 These things I command you, that ye love one another." John 15:8-17.

Peace comes from being in Love with God.

"Great peace have they which love thy law: and nothing shall offend them." Psalm 119:165

"Finally, brethren, farewell. Be perfect, be of good comfort, be of one mind, live in peace; and the God of love and peace shall be with you." 2 Corinthians 13:11.

Patience and **kindness** are characteristics of love. "Love is patient and love is kind..." 1 Corinthians 13:4.

Goodness is found in love. "(For the fruit of the Spirit is in all goodness and righteousness and truth;)" Ephesians 5:9.

Faithfulness is characteristic of the God who is love.
"For great is his steadfast love toward us; and the faithfulness of the Lord endures forever." Psalm 117:2

Gentleness: "Shall I come ... in love in the spirit of gentleness." 1 Corinthians 4:21.

Self-control: "For God did not give us a spirit of fear, but of power and love and self-control." 1 Timothy 1:7.

Love is Found in Every Kind of Scripture

We have already seen love in the law. It also shows up in history.

David's love for Jonathan: "I am distressed for thee, my brother Jonathan: very pleasant hast thou been unto me: thy love to me was wonderful, passing the love of women." 2 Samuel 1:26.

David's love for God: "I love the LORD, because he hath heard my voice and my supplications." Psalm 116:1.

Solomon's love for God: "And Solomon loved the LORD, walking in the statutes of David his father: only he sacrificed and burnt incense in high places." 1 Kings 3:3.

God's love for David: "And when he had removed him, he raised up unto them David to be their king; to whom also he gave testimony, and said, I have found David the son of Jesse, a man after mine own heart, which shall fulfil all my will." Acts 13:22.

God's love for Israel: "7 The LORD did not set his love upon you, nor choose you, because ye were more in number than any people; for ye were the fewest of all people: 8 But because the LORD loved you, and because he would keep the oath which he had sworn unto your fathers, hath the LORD brought you out with a mighty hand, and redeemed you out of the house of bondmen, from the hand of Pharaoh king of Egypt." Deuteronomy 7:7-8

Israel's love for God: "But take diligent heed to do the commandment and the law, which Moses the servant of the LORD charged you, to love the LORD your God, and to walk in all his ways, and to keep his commandments, and to cleave unto him, and to serve him with all your heart and with all your soul." Joshua 22:5.

Love is in the Word's Poetry

The Song of Solomon is the highest form of Scripture poetry about love. We will talk at length about the Song of Solomon later. Psalms also contain great love poetry. As you read through Psalms, watching for it, you can't help but observe deep, intense love.

God's love for us: "Yet the LORD will command his lovingkindness in the daytime, and in the night his song shall be with me, and my prayer unto the God of my life." Psalm 42:8.

"How excellent is thy lovingkindness, O God! therefore the children of men put their trust under the shadow of thy wings." Psalm 36:7.

"The LORD openeth the eyes of the blind: the LORD raiseth them that are bowed down: the LORD loveth the righteous:" Psalm 146:8.

David's love for God: "Because thy lovingkindness is better than life, my lips shall praise Thee." Psalm 63:3.

Love is in the Wisdom Literature

"For whom the LORD loveth he correcteth; even as a father the son in whom he delighteth." Proverbs 3:12.

"I love them that love me; and those that seek me early shall find me." Proverbs 8:17.

"Hatred stirreth up strifes: but love covereth all sins." Proverbs 10:12.

"A friend loveth at all times, and a brother is born for adversity." Proverbs 17:17.

"My son, give me thine heart, and let thine eyes observe my ways." Proverbs 23:26.

Love is Seen in the Prophets

Demonstrated love is the basis for healing and answered prayer: "1 Cry aloud, spare not, lift up thy voice like a trumpet, and show my people their transgression, and the house of Jacob their sins. 2 Yet they seek me daily, and delight to know my ways, as a nation that did righteousness, and forsook not the ordinance of their God: they ask of me the ordinances of justice; they take delight in approaching to God. 3 Wherefore have we fasted, say they, and thou seest not? wherefore have we afflicted our soul, and thou takest no knowledge? Behold, in the day of your fast ye find pleasure, and exact all your labours. 4 Behold, ye fast for strife and debate, and to smite with the fist of wickedness: ye shall not fast as ye do this day, to make your voice to be heard on high. 5 Is it such a fast that I have chosen? a day for a man to afflict his soul? is it to bow down his head as a bulrush, and to spread sackcloth and ashes under him? wilt thou call this a fast, and an acceptable day to the LORD? 6 Is not this the fast that I have chosen? to loose the bands of wickedness, to undo the heavy burdens, and to let the oppressed go free, and that ye break every yoke? 7 Is it not to deal thy bread to the hungry, and that thou bring the poor that are cast out to thy house? when thou seest the naked, that thou cover him; and that thou hide not thyself from thine own flesh? 8 Then shall thy light break forth as the morning, and thine health shall spring forth speedily: and thy righteousness shall go before thee; the glory of the LORD shall be thy reward. 9 Then shalt thou call, and the LORD shall answer; thou shalt cry, and he shall say, Here I am. If thou take away from the midst of thee the yoke, the putting forth of the finger, and speaking vanity; 10 And if thou draw out thy soul to the hungry, and satisfy the afflicted soul; then shall thy light rise in obscurity, and thy darkness be as the noon day: 11 And the LORD shall guide thee continually, and satisfy thy soul in drought, and make fat thy bones: and thou shalt be like a watered garden, and like a spring of water, whose waters fail not. 12 And they that shall be of thee shall build the old waste places: thou shalt raise up the foundations of many generations; and thou shalt be called, The repairer of the breach, The restorer of paths to dwell in." Isaiah 58:1-12.

We can come before the Lord, if we love: "6 Wherewith shall I come before the LORD, and bow myself before the high God? shall I come before him with burnt offerings, with calves of a year old? 7 Will the LORD be pleased with thousands of rams, or with ten thousands of rivers of oil? shall I give my first-born for my transgression, the fruit of my body for the sin of my soul? 8 He hath showed thee, O man, what is good; and what doth the LORD require of thee, but to do justly, and to love mercy, and to walk humbly with thy God?" Micah 6:6-8

God's love for Israel: "In all their affliction he was afflicted, and the angel of his presence saved them: in his love and in his pity he redeemed them; and he bare them, and carried them all the days of old." Isaiah 63:9.

"The LORD hath appeared of old unto me, saying, Yea, I have loved thee with an everlasting love: therefore with lovingkindness have I drawn thee." Jeremiah 31:3.

The prophet speaks against those who love with their mouths, but not with their hearts: "31 And they come unto thee as the people cometh, and they sit before thee as my people, and they hear thy words, but they will not do them: for with their mouth they show much love, but their heart goeth after their covetousness. 32 And, lo, thou art unto them as a very lovely song of one that hath a pleasant voice, and can play well on an instrument: for they hear thy words, but they do them not." Ezekiel 33:31-32.

God's love for all who love Him: "5 Even unto them will I give in mine house and within my walls a place and a name better than of sons and of daughters: I will give them an everlasting name, that shall not be cut off. 6 Also the sons of the stranger, that join themselves to the LORD, to serve him, and to love the name of the LORD, to be his servants, every one that keepeth the sabbath from polluting it, and taketh hold of my covenant;" Isaiah 56:5-6.

Love is Seen in the Gospels

We have already seen the New Testament commandments to love. We see love in other ways in the Gospels.

God's love for us: "16 For God so loved the world, that he gave his only begotten Son, that whosoever believeth in him should not perish, but have everlasting life. 17 For God sent not his Son into the world to condemn the world; but that the world through him might be saved." John 3:16-17.

Love is in the doing, not just in the saying: "21 He that hath my commandments, and keepeth them, he it is that loveth me: and he that loveth me shall be loved of my Father, and I will love him, and will manifest myself to him. ... 23 Jesus answered and said unto him, If a man love me, he will keep my words: and my Father will love him, and we will come unto him, and make our abode with him." John 14:21,23.

"But woe unto you, Pharisees! for ye tithe mint and rue and all manner of herbs, and pass over judgment and the love of God: these ought ye to have done, and not to leave the other undone." Luke 11:42.

"15 If ye love me, keep my commandments." John 14:15.

Love is Found throughout the New Testament Letters

"But God commendeth his love toward us, in that, while we were yet sinners, Christ died for us." Romans 5:8.

"But if any man love God, the same is known of him." 1 Corinthians 8:3.

"If any man love not the Lord Jesus Christ, let him be Anathema Maranatha." 1 Corinthians 16:22.

In 1 Corinthians 12, God talks to us about the gifts of power. He ends that chapter by saying "But covet earnestly the best gifts: and yet show I unto you a more excellent way." He goes on to give us a passage of scripture that even the unsaved call beautiful:

"1 Though I speak with the tongues of men and of angels, and have not love, I am become as sounding brass, or a tinkling cymbal. 2 And though I have the gift of prophecy, and understand all mysteries, and all knowledge; and though I have all faith, so that I could remove mountains, and have not love, I am nothing. 3 And though I bestow all my goods to feed the poor, and though I give my body to be burned, and have not love, it profiteth me nothing. 4 love suffereth long, and is kind; love envieth not; love vaunteth not itself, is not puffed up, 5 Doth not behave itself unseemly, seeketh not her own, is not easily provoked, thinketh no evil; 6 Rejoiceth not in iniquity, but rejoiceth in the truth; 7 Beareth all things, believeth all things, hopeth all things, endureth all things. 8 love never faileth: but whether there be prophecies, they shall fail; whether there be tongues, they shall cease; whether there be knowledge, it shall vanish away. 9 For we know in part, and we prophesy in part. 10 But when that which is perfect is come, then that which is in part shall be done away. 11 When I was a child, I spake as a child, I understood as a child, I thought as a child: but when I became a man, I put away childish things. 12 For now we see through a glass, darkly; but then face to face: now I know in part; but then shall I know even as also I am known. 13 And now abideth faith, hope, love, these three; but the greatest of these is love."

In Chapter 14, verse 1, He puts the power and love together in order: "Follow after love, and desire spiritual gifts, but rather that ye may prophesy."

John, the Beloved, gives us a glimpse of the love that consumed him: "7 Beloved, let us love one another: for love is of God; and every one that loveth is born of God, and knoweth God. 8 He that loveth not knoweth not God; for God is love. 9 In this was manifested the love of God toward us, because that God sent his only begotten Son into the world, that we might live through him. 10 Herein is love, not that we loved God, but that he loved us, and sent his Son to be the propitiation for our sins.

11 Beloved, if God so loved us, we ought also to love one another. 12 No man hath seen God at any time. If we love one another, God dwelleth in us, and his love is perfected in us. 13 Hereby know we that we dwell in him, and he in us, because he hath given us of his Spirit. 14 And we have seen and do testify that the Father sent the Son to be the Saviour of the world. 15 Whosoever shall confess that Jesus is the Son of God, God dwelleth in him, and he in God. 16 And we have known and believed the love that God hath to us. God is love; and he that dwelleth in love dwelleth in God, and God in him. 17 Herein is our love made perfect, that we may have boldness in the day of judgment: because as he is, so are we in this world. 18 There is no fear in love; but perfect love casteth out fear: because fear hath torment. He that feareth is not made perfect in love. 19 We love him, because he first loved us. 20 If a man say, I love God, and hateth his brother, he is a liar: for he that loveth not his brother whom he hath seen, how can he love God whom he hath not seen? 21 And this commandment have we from him, That he who loveth God love his brother also." 1 John 4:7-21.

Every kind of Scripture, every part of Scripture, crossing the bounds of gift, law, commandment, fruit, nature of God, etc.; love is the message, love is the meaning, love is the reason, love is the purpose, love is the goal. Love is the reason for the Bible, the creation, you, humanity, redemption, and Jesus.

It's All About Loving Him!

We have made it about everything but **love**. We need to make it ALL about **love**.

CHAPTER TWO

HOW FAR WILL YOU GO?

Everyone has some fear of *intimacy*. The further I allow you into me, the more power I give you to hurt me. That is why we fear "*into me, see*"? This fear of intimacy interferes with marriage, friendship, honesty, and openness.

In marriage, people often sabotage intimacy whenever they begin to get too close or things begin to go too good. I had a counselee who said that she was terribly uncomfortable in my presence because she felt as though I could see into her soul! Intimacy with God is even scarier! In Genesis 3:8, Adam and Eve heard the sound of God walking in the garden and they hid themselves because they knew that they were naked. We are no different than them. We are afraid that God will see our sin and destroy us because of our guilt.

In Exodus, Chapter 20, the people got tired of Moses going up to the mountain and hearing from God. They wanted to hear God for themselves. After consecrating themselves, they gathered around the mountain to meet with God. As He descended to speak with them, they ran away in fear. In verse 19, they told Moses to go up and talk with God and come again and tell them what He said. They did not want God to speak to them, lest He kill them.

This is GOD! He is Almighty, Eternal, Omnipresent, Omniscient, and He is the Final Ultimate Judge! The power of eternal life and death are in His hand! There is every reason to be afraid of God. But, thanks be to God, that through Jesus, we have entrance into God. In fact, we are told in Hebrews 4:16 "to come boldly before the throne of grace."

We are also told in 1 John 4:18 that "perfect love casts out all fear" of punishment!

So, how far into the Lord will you go? How much are you willing to risk? How much of Him do you desire to experience?

In Christ

In English, the work "IN" means any place within the Circle. The "X" is in the circle. In Greek the word "EN," which is translated "IN," means "in the center of." The "C" is "EN" the circle. To be "in Christ" means to be "in the center of Christ." Most American Christians are trying to see how far out they can go and still be "in" Christ. God is looking for those who are trying to see how far "EN" Christ we can be.

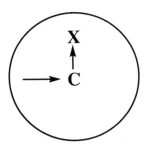

Elijah Passes on the Mantle

Before passing on the mantle to Elisha, Elijah wanted to see how far Elisha would go. In 2 Kings 2, Elijah repeatedly tells Elisha to "wait here" while he goes on ahead. Elisha keeps insisting that he is going all the way. Because he did go all the way, he got to see Elijah raptured. He also requested and received a double portion of Elijah's mantle. There are actually more miracles attributed to Elisha than to Elijah!

Along our journey into the Lord, there are many opportunities to rest or stop. Most people think that they have all they want or need of God. They are comfortable that they are saved. They know how to pray. They occasionally actually see prayers answered. They may have seen people healed, or delivered.

They believe that they are OK with God. They may not know that there even is more! They may have never heard of miracles, two-way conversations with God, answered prayer, or intimacy with God.

Most people who know that more is possible, also know that to go further will require a higher price from them. They expect that God may actually begin to interfere with their comfortable lifestyle. So, to them, there are negatives attached to going further into Christ.

How far will you go? How far into Jesus do you want to go? How deeply in love with Him do you want to be? If you have all you want, then stay where you are. You'll be fine there. As for me, I will go on ahead. I want to go as far a God allows!

Statistics

Statisticians use something called a bell curve. It is used to describe the way groups of people break down into categories. Any given population is expected to break down into groups of 10%, 80%, and 10%. The upper and lower 10% represent the bottom right and left flare-out of the curve. The 80% represent the main body of the bell curve. If we apply this bell curve to the people in your church, the top 10% will do 90% of the work and will give 90% of the tithes and offerings. The next 80% of the people will produce 10% of the work and will give 10% of all the offerings given. The last 10% of the people will do and give nothing. Look around your church. Is this not true? Ask your pastor.

Ten percent of the people will not love the Lord at all. Eighty percent of the people will give the Lord 10% of the love He is going to receive. Ten percent of the people will give Him 90% of the love He will receive. That top ten percent of Christians will enter into a deep, intimate love relationship with Jesus.

Look at the Disciples

Now let's move the bell curve to a different set of people. We will move from the general population of Christians to the unique group of the disciples. They, too, break down into a bell curve of 10-80-10. One of them betrayed Jesus and was clearly not in love with Him. He represents the bottom ten percent. Ten of them loved and served the Lord. They represent the eighty percent. One disciple, John the Beloved, loved Him deeply, intimately. He was the one who laid his head on Jesus' chest at the Last Supper.

Jesus and John were mature, straight, adult males. Yet, John was so intimately in love with Jesus that he was laying his head on Jesus' chest, in front of the others. He was the only one who acted this way. He is called John the Beloved. He refers to himself in the Gospel of John as *the* disciple whom Jesus loved.

The deepest love relationship between two men in the Scriptures was between David and Jonathan. David declared that his love for Jonathan surpassed the love of a woman! Jonathon and David were both mature straight males. Interestingly, Jesus is called the "Son of David" and "John" is a form of "Jonathan." The Old Testament relationship was a foretaste the relationship between Jesus and John.

John the Beloved wrote five books of the New Testament. It was to John that Jesus gave the Revelation. One of his books, 1 John, is heavily devoted to the subject of love: God's love for us, our love for Him, and the requirement of our love for the brethren. John was a top ten percenter.

The Love of God does not Speak of the Value of the Individual

Pride and ego have no place in the love of God. Some people, with a religious spirit, press into the deeper things to see how spiritual *they* can get. The more they learn and accomplish, the more prideful, arrogant, and judgmental they become. The more they learn, the more they elevate themselves. These things are evidence that their professed love of Jesus is not genuine. It is lust, not love. It is self-seeking and self-serving, not Christ-seeking and Christ-serving. It elevates self rather than elevating the Lord. The more we truly love Jesus, the more we die to self!

26

Such self-seeking was even found amongst the disciples: "20 Then came to him the mother of Zebedee's children with her sons, worshipping him, and desiring a certain thing of him. 21 And he said unto her, What wilt thou? She saith unto him, Grant that these my two sons may sit, the one on thy right hand, and the other on the left, in thy kingdom. 22 But Jesus answered and said, Ye know not what ye ask. Are ye able to drink of the cup that I shall drink of, and to be baptized with the baptism that I am baptized with? They say unto him, We are able. 23 And he saith unto them, Ye shall drink indeed of my cup, and be baptized with the baptism that I am baptized with: but to sit on my right hand, and on my left, is not mine to give, but it shall be given to them for whom it is prepared of my Father." Matthew 20:20-23.

The fact that one grows in spiritual knowledge and even in prayer does not give them cause to think themselves of more value than that of newer believers or those who have chosen not to press in. The fact that John was called The Beloved, does not make him of any greater value to the Kingdom than the other disciples. They changed the world, saved souls, enlarged the church, wrote, preached, taught, prayed, worked miracles, etc. God loved them no less than He loved John. He simply loved them differently.

Jesus shows us that He accepted the limited amount of love that the disciples were able to give to Him. Before we can fully understand the Word, we need to understand the language.

Words of Love

The New Testament Greek language uses three different words to express love.

AGAPE is the highest form of love. It is used to speak of God's love. It is used to speak of love as a choice. It desires to seek the best for others. It seeks nothing for itself. The King James Version of the Bible translated this word as "charity." The intent is to express love that *does* something. It is self-sacrificing. It is the willingness to serve the other at our personal expense. It has been called love with work clothes on.

This is the love that Jesus had for John. This is the love He had for the rest of the disciples. This is the love He has for you! This is the love with which we are commanded to love one another. (John 15:12) Jesus said that if the disciples loved Him with this kind of love, they would have rejoiced when He told them He was going to the Father. (John 14:28)

PHILIOS is brotherly affection. This is the true caring of the soul. It speaks of the love of good friends. It is the kind of love that the disciples had for Jesus. It is not quite as self-sacrificing as *AGAPE*.

STORGE is family affection, parents for children and children for parents.

There is another Greek word for love that is not found in the Bible. It is *EROS*. This is physical, romantic love. This is **NOT** the kind of love demonstrated by David, Jonathan, Jesus or John.

Now, let's look at the scripture:

John 21:15-19

"15 So when they had dined, Jesus saith to Simon Peter, Simon, son of Jonas, lovest thou me more than these? He saith unto him, Yea, Lord; thou knowest that I love thee. He saith unto him, Feed my lambs. 16 He saith to him again the second time, Simon, son of Jonas, lovest thou me? He saith unto him, Yea, Lord; thou knowest that I love thee. He saith unto him, Feed my sheep. 17 He saith unto him the third time, Simon, son of Jonas, lovest thou me? Peter was grieved because he said unto him the third time, Lovest thou me? And he said unto him, Lord, thou knowest all things; thou knowest that I love thee. Jesus saith unto him, Feed my sheep. 18 Verily, verily, I say unto thee, When thou wast young, thou girdedst thyself, and walkedst whither thou wouldest: but when thou shalt be old, thou shalt stretch forth thy hands, and another shall gird thee, and carry thee whither thou wouldest not. 19 This spake he, signifying by what death he should glorify God. And when he had spoken this, he saith unto him, Follow me."

At first glance, we see Jesus asking Peter three times if he loves Him. When we look at the Greek, it looks like this:

John 21:15-19

"15 So when they had dined, Jesus saith to Simon Peter, Simon, son of Jonas, lovest *AGAPE* thou me more than these? He saith unto him, Yea, Lord; thou knowest that I love *PHILIOS* thee. He saith unto him, Feed my lambs. 16 He saith to him again the second time, Simon, son of Jonas, lovest *AGAPE* thou me? He saith unto him, Yea, Lord; thou knowest that I love *PHILIOS* thee. He saith unto him, Feed my sheep. 17 He saith unto him the third time, Simon, son of Jonas, lovest *PHILIOS* thou me? Peter was grieved because he said unto him the third time, Lovest *PHILIOS* thou me? And he said unto him, Lord, thou knowest all things; thou knowest that I love *PHILIOS* thee. Jesus saith unto him, Feed my sheep. 18 Verily, verily, I say unto thee, When thou wast young, thou girdedst thyself, and walkedst whither thou wouldest: but when thou shalt be old, thou shalt stretch forth thy hands, and another shall gird thee, and carry thee whither thou wouldest not. 19 This spake he, signifying by what death he should glorify God. And when he had spoken this, he saith unto him, Follow me."

Jesus had reason to question Peter's love. Peter had just recently denied that he even knew Him. Jesus was giving Peter the opportunity to clarify for himself that he really did love the Lord. Jesus was asking Peter for the deepest, highest form of love. Peter responded that he loved Jesus, but not quite that much. The second time Jesus asked the question the same way and got the same answer. The third time, Jesus lowered His expectation by asking Peter if he *Philiosed* Him. He was also asking Peter to check himself to see if that was really true. Peter confirmed that he did love Jesus with brotherly love. Jesus accepted his offering. It was the best that Peter could give. Jesus did not judge him inadequate, even though John loved Him with a deeper kind of love. Jesus gave Peter his directions and ultimately would tell Peter that He would be the foundation stone of the church.

It was right before this passage in verses three through eight that Jesus blessed Peter's fishing. At the time of Peter's call, he was told to leave his nets and become a fisher of men, which he did. Now, with Jesus "gone," Peter goes back to fishing. Jesus shows His love by giving Peter a catch so big he needed help getting it into the boat.

But What About Him?

As soon a Jesus had accepted Peter's less than best commitment and given him his assignment, Peter immediately asked what was going to happen to John the Beloved. He was probably wondering if John was going to be treated better than he. Jesus answer was basically: "What business is that of yours?"

What is this Deeper Love?

Maybe you have had no idea that a deeper love of the Lord was possible. We read the words, but words mean different things to us based on our experience. Maybe you have no clue what kind of love God wants to give to you or what kind of love He wants to receive from you. Maybe you have no idea what it would be like. Maybe you desire more but don't know how to attain it. Read on.

CHAPTER THREE

THE PRACTICE OF
THE PRESENCE OF GOD

In the middle of the 1600's there was a priest named Brother Lawrence from the Lorraine region of France. He was an insignificant monk in a monastery. Yet his book *The Practice of the Presence of God* has become a spiritual classic that has inspired many a seeker. Brother Lawrence wanted more. He wanted to go further, not so that he could be somebody, but that he could be "a nobody" for Jesus. He didn't want to *do* something. He wanted to *be* something: a lover of Jesus.

Brother Lawrence listened to all the advice from his knowledgeable superiors and he attempted to follow their instructions. Each time, it led to emptiness and futility. His attempts to go deeper into the Lord met with guilt, shame, and condemnation from the Evil One. He had to fight the mental battle to stand in the grace that is ours through the Blood of The Lamb.

He finally determined just to accept the love of the Lord and to love the Lord; to express that love, to walk in that love and to practice the presence of God. His level of fellowship with Jesus is now legendary.

He came to see everything that was not God as a distraction. He encouraged others to seek and take pleasure in nothing but God. At the same time, he encouraged others not to become legalistic about abandoning the distractions of life. He encouraged them to remember that God will accept whatever level of dedication we choose to offer. (Salvation is by grace not works.)

Brother Lawrence learned how to abide in the presence of God all the time, through good and bad, pain and blessing, joy and sorrow.

The Word

Consider the following scriptures:

"And the LORD, he it is that doth go before thee; he will be with thee, he will not fail thee, neither forsake thee: fear not, neither be dismayed." Deuteronomy 31:8.

"Have not I commanded thee? Be strong and of a good courage; be not afraid, neither be thou dismayed: for the LORD thy God is with thee whithersoever thou goest."
Joshua 1:9.

"7 Whither shall I go from thy spirit? or whither shall I flee from thy presence? 8 If I ascend up into heaven, thou art there: if I make my bed in hell, behold, thou art there.
9 If I take the wings of the morning, and dwell in the uttermost parts of the sea; 10 Even there shall thy hand lead me, and thy right hand shall hold me." Psalm 139:7-10.

"...for he hath said, I will never leave thee, nor forsake thee." Hebrews 13:5b.

The Names

Consider some of the Old Testament Hebrew Names of God:

V'Lo Elohey Merachok	The God who not far off. Jeremiah 23:23.
Elohey Mikarov	The God who is near. Jeremiah 23:23.
Yehovah Immach	Jehovah is with you. 2 Samuel 7:3.
Elohim Immach	God is with you. 1 Samuel 10:7.
Imcha Ani	I Am with you. Isaiah 41:10.

Do you Really Believe?

Do you believe that this is the true Word of God?
If you did really believe it, how would you act?

   If God were right there with you, would you be afraid of
      anything?
   If God were right there with you, would you be so free to do
      things that were offensive to Him?
   If God were right there with you, would you feel lonely?
   If God were right there with you, would you ignore Him?
Do you act like you believe that God is with you wherever you go?

Most Christians would have to answer that they do not act like they REALLY believe that God is with them wherever they go. Yet He is not only with you, He is IN you!

"9 But ye are not in the flesh, but in the Spirit, if so be that the Spirit of God dwell in you. Now if any man have not the Spirit of Christ, he is none of his.10 And if Christ be in you, the body is dead because of sin; but the Spirit is life because of righteousness. 11 But if the Spirit of him that raised up Jesus from the dead dwell in you, he that raised up Christ from the dead shall also quicken your mortal bodies by his Spirit that dwelleth in you." Romans 8:9-11.

"...for ye are the temple of the living God; as God hath said, I will dwell in them, and walk in them; and I will be their God, and they shall be my people." 2 Corinthians 6:16b.

"17 That Christ may dwell in your hearts by faith; that ye, being rooted and grounded in love, 18 May be able to comprehend with all saints what is the breadth, and length, and depth, and height; 19 And to know the love of Christ, which passeth knowledge, that ye might be filled with all the fulness of God." Ephesians 3:17-19.

The God Hunt

About fifteen years ago, there was a radio program out of Canada that had a great impact on many. They invited people to go on a Lenten journey. The call was to go on a "God Hunt."

The premise was this: if God is really with us all the time then we should seek to experience His presence. As I remember it, the format was fairly simple. Each day searchers would meditate on scripture that spoke of God's presence and active participation in our lives. They would pray that God would reveal Himself; that He would help the searcher to listen for His voice, watch for His hand, and seek the guidance of His Spirit. Instead of seeing things as coincidence, they were encouraged to expect to see God act. They were to listen for that still small voice. They were to watch for God manipulating circumstances. Each evening, they would journal what they had experienced. There was also Bible study associated with the presence of God.

By the end of the study, the searchers had clearly experienced the presence of God! All doubt was removed. For those who wanted to go deeper, they had developed a sound foundation for that journey.

God Stories

Many of us have God stories, events in which God dramatically intervened. One lady told me of a night when God woke her up, pulled her by the arm into another room to show her a smoldering fire about to ignite.

A counselee told me about driving an eighteen wheel moving van down a steep winding mountain road. He heard someone yell "STOP!" He shook his head and questioned his sanity. Again he heard "I SAID, STOP!!!!" This time he stopped abruptly at a sharp curve. Right on the far side of the curve, a family in a station wagon had spun out and was sideways in the road. Had he of ignored the command, he would have surely killed the entire family.

One day, while entering an intersection, I inexplicably stepped on the brake. An instant later, a speeding car blew through the opposing red light at about 95 MPH followed by several police cars. I had not heard sirens, because I had the worship music cranked up on my radio. I had not seen the speeding vehicles; at that speed they were a great distance from the intersection when I stopped. Why did I stop? God, of course.

These are significant events. Yet, every day, all day, God is actively working on our behalf. His is speaking, leading, guiding, directing, and convicting. We not only ignore Him; we often make excuses to deny His presence.

Presence Leads to Obedience

If God's presence is that real, then He is able to show us His will and direct our steps. If He is able to do that, then we must be willing to *allow* Him to direct or steps.

How far will you go? Brother Lawrence got to the point that he would not do a thing without the assurance of the Lord's approval. That is how Jesus acted.

"19 Then answered Jesus and said unto them, Verily, verily, I say unto you, The Son can do nothing of himself, but what he seeth the Father do: for what things soever he doeth, these also doeth the Son likewise. 20 For the Father loveth the Son, and showeth him all things that himself doeth: and he will show him greater works than these, that ye may marvel." John 5:19-20.

How far will you go?

The God Hunt

I challenge you to go on a "God Hunt." Seek His presence. Seek His voice. Seek His hand. Seek His will. Watch. Listen. Observe.

CHAPTER FOUR

FOR WHAT?

For what reason are you seeking God? For what are you hoping?

The Pittsburgh Revival

Years ago, we were in revival when the steel industry collapsed in Pittsburgh, Pennsylvania. Many steel workers who lost their jobs, plopped down on the couch and popped open a can of beer, and never moved. They may still be there. Others came to church, seeking God. They were highly motivated, broken and hurting. They witnessed the Glory of God.

The anointing was so strong that people were sovereignly saved, healed and delivered during worship. Blind eyes were opened. The deaf heard. The demonized were delivered. People left their braces and walkers to be mounted on our "Jesus' trophy wall" in the sanctuary. People laid prostrate on the floor, knelt, wept, sang, danced, shouted, sang in the spirit for extended periods of time. Sometimes, we just stood in silence in the awesome presence of God. I used to joke that we could read from the phone book and people would get saved. Dozens were saved at each service.

Many steel workers were wonderfully, miraculously saved. The body then stepped up and found them jobs. It wouldn't be long before they stopped coming to church. They had what they wanted. It was not God. It was a job.

The God Chasers

I recently was thrilled to read *THE GOD CHASERS*, by Tommy Tenny. I loved the hunger. I thrilled at the miraculous encounters. But, I was left with a lingering question: For what is he really seeking?

I, too, long for the Power and the Glory. I, too, long to see God glorified in His body. I long to see the lost saved. I long for true repentance and revival! I long to see God show up in His "*awe full*" Majesty. LORD, PLEASE BRING IT NOW!!!!!!!!!!!! I, too, long to taste and see the outpouring! Revival is His heart. Salvation and repentance is His desire!

But, what of the decades, even the centuries, in between revivals? What if it doesn't come before we die? What of all those generations who lived without a major revival?

What does it mean to chase after God? Is He running away from us? Is He hiding from us? What would we do with Him if we caught Him? I have never known God to run from those who truly desire to love Him. He simply seeks to find out if our pursuit is really motivated by love or if we are seeking our own desires. Many are seeking the experience, rather than seeking His face.

When God brought me to Phoenix, I thought that I was coming here to help with the revival. God had other ideas. He brought me here to seek His face and become His lover.

1 Corinthians 14:1 tells us to "Make love our aim and sincerely desire the higher gifts." Balance is required, but the priority is clear. Love is to be the aim. Not the sound and the fury, not the revival, not the miracles, not the demonstration of His power. By all means desire those things! By all means have a passion for the lost. But, make love your aim! To love Him is what it is all about. You can love Him when no one else does. You can love Him when there has not been a revival for centuries. You can love Him when the rest of the world hates Him! Loving Him will sustain you in between revivals. Loving Him will motivate you to desire revival. But, the purpose of revival is to draw people to love Him!

The word "holy" in the Greek is *agios*. It is literally translated "set apart for." The question is "set apart for" what? The answer is, set apart to love the Lord. What is it all about? What is it all for?

There is a worship song that encourages us to "seek the giver not the gift." We also need to seek the one who brings revival, not the revival itself, or revival becomes an end in itself.

Love vs. Lust

Love has a desire to give and bless the other. Lust has the desire to get the other to give or bless me. Most of our Christian experience is directed at getting God to do what we want! I need. I want. I beg You to... I fast to gain Your favor and get my prayer answered. I learn faith to accomplish what I want. Our "worship services" even serve the needs and desires of the body. They do not seek to minister to Him! ALL OF THIS IS LUST!

Love seeks to bless God and minister to Him. Love seeks to find out what is pleasing to Him. "Try to learn what is pleasing to the Lord." [Ephesians 5:10 RSV.] Love seeks to serve Him. What do You want, Lord? What do You desire me to do? In love, prayer is about Him. Worship is about Him. Ministry is about Him. Vision is about Him. The body is about Him.

In love, we speak love to Him. We sing love to Him. We act in love to Him. We make love to Him.

Balance

Balance is the key to life. Balance brings health. Anything that gets out of balance gets sick. Balance is dependent on priority.

When God says: "Make love your aim and sincerely desire the higher gifts" 1 Corinthians 14:1, He gives us a priority. If we seek only the love of God, we miss the love of man and love of the brethren. We become "so heavenly minded that we are no earthly good."

When the disciples witnessed the transfiguration, they wanted to build a tabernacle. They wanted to stay there. Who wouldn't want to stay after experiencing what they did? Jesus would not let them stay or build a tabernacle. He brought them down from the mountain. Immediately upon descending, they were engulfed in ministry.

Balance is the key. If all I want to do is love the Lord, I will lock myself away from the world. I might just as well die, and go home and love Him in Heaven, because I am of no value here. Paul realized this truth. He said "for me to live is Christ, for me to die is gain". Philippians1:21. To live serves God's purpose. To die is the blessing to which we all look forward. It is the fulfillment of His love for us, and our love for Him.

Balance must be maintained in the other direction as well. To seek after the effect, produce, or harvest, puts us out of balance. Love is the aim. What that love accomplishes here on the earth is secondary. Remember, the whole purpose of creation was for us to love the Lord. It is our first and great commandment. The whole purpose of revival is to call others to love Him.

CHAPTER FIVE

THE SONG OF SONGS

The Song of Solomon is a very unique book in the Bible. It is unique because it is so totally different than the other books of the Bible. It is a love poem. It is beautiful, intriguing, sensitive, romantic, passionate, intense, and inspiring. It is so steamy that when I have read it aloud in mixed company, I have seen married adults blush and giggle uncomfortably. It is held up as an example of Godly love in a Christian marriage. But it is so much more.

While it is usually entitled the Song of Solomon, its original title was the Song of Songs, meaning the highest song possible. Its lowest level of meaning, speaks about marital love. Its has two higher levels which speak of God's love relationship with Israel, of Christ and His Bride, the Church. However, its highest meaning is the love relationship between Jesus and the individual believer.

It is so unique that some experts boldly proclaim that it has no place in the canon of scripture. It is hard to find experts who agree as to its meaning and interpretation. As we read some authorities, it becomes clear that they are clueless about this intense love relationship with Jesus.

The book is difficult to interpret, if you try to break it down line by line. However, if we remember that it is a love song and poetic in nature, we can allow it to paint a beautiful picture for us.

Before you proceed to read this chapter, please take time to read the entire book of the Song of Solomon. There are only eight short chapters, so it is no problem to read quickly. It is first scripture in Part Two of this book. When you are ready to proceed, I recommend that you have at least two versions of scripture at hand to help as you consider this difficult passage of scripture. Please pray that God will open you heart and that you "May be able to comprehend with all the saints what is the breadth, and length, and depth, and height; And to know the love of Christ, which passeth knowledge, that ye might be filled with all the fullness of God." Ephesians 3:18-19.

Try to keep an open mind, for few have seen their love of Jesus in these terms! It is especially difficult for men to see themselves as the Bride of Christ. Try to hear what God is really saying in these verses.

Commentary

Now let's consider what you have just read. This is Solomon's highest offering. It is above all else. It is more than life itself.

Chapter 1

In the first few verses the bride who represents Israel, the Bride of Christ, and the individual believer awaits her lover. She asks to be drawn after Him. She is not driven to Him, she is drawn to Him.

We are drawn to the Lord, not driven. "We love because He first loved us." 1 John 4:19 We are drawn to love the Lord because He has poured out His love on us. Those of us who press in are inexplicable drawn to do so. We are filled with passion and desire. We hunger for it!

Even His Name is as ointment poured forth. His Name brings healing and a beautiful fragrance. Verse 3.

The King, Jesus, has brought us into His chambers. We have been brought into God's presence by the Blood of the Lamb. Because of the Blood we may enter boldly into His presence. (Hebrews 4:16)

In verses 5-6 of this first chapter, the betrothed, the bride, the lover refers to herself as dark like the tanned cloth of the tents of Kedar [the decedents of Ishmael]: meaning that she is sinful, unacceptable. She was required to tend the vineyard, but she failed to attend to her own life.

Yet, her lover sees her as "the fairest of women." Verse 8. We have been washed, cleansed, justified and sanctified by the Blood. (1 Corinthians 6:11) We are new creatures in Christ. (2 Corinthians 5:17.) In verse 10, He calls her beautiful and notes that she is adorned with jewels. These are jewels that He has given her. We become beautiful because of His Blood, presence, grace, and Spirit.

Her lover then proceeds to praise her and adore her! Did you know that God praises you and rejoices over you? He does. "The LORD thy God in the midst of thee is mighty; he will save, he will rejoice over thee with joy; he will rest in his love, he will joy over thee with singing." Zephaniah 3:17.

"For as a young man marrieth a virgin, so shall thy sons marry thee: and as the bridegroom rejoiceth over the bride, so shall thy God rejoice over thee." Isaiah 62:5.

There is a place in the Lord where we begin to hear the Lord singing over us and speaking His love and approval for us. We do not need to wait until we enter His rest to hear "Well done." His love songs are incredibly beautiful. His affirmation of His love for us is awesome. His words of love are healing to our souls.

Look at the way He speaks to you here in His Song. These are passionate words of intense love. He desires you! He wants you! If you become intimate with Him you will hear Him say these things to you.

In verse 7 she asks how to find Him. She remarks that she should not be distracted and drawn aside like His other companions. Even if she were with them, she would have to hide herself from them. But if she is with her lover, she can be unveiled!

He responds in verse 8 that she should know the way. She should follow His tracks and camp next to Him. After all, He is the Way! "5 Thomas saith unto him, Lord, we know not whither thou goest; and how can we know the way? 6 Jesus saith unto him, I am the way, the truth, and the life: no man cometh unto the Father, but by me." John 14:5-6. God told the Israelites in the wilderness to camp when He said "camp" and move when He moved.

Chapter 2

In Chapter 2, they take turns honoring, praising, and desiring one another. The passion and desire are great. We are encouraged not to stir up love until we are ready to enter in. I can relate to this. My passion for the love of the Lord was stirred up long before I was ready to enter in. My heart has longed and ached for this deep intimacy! I felt the deep emptiness and gut-wrenching hunger. I can't imagine what our God of love suffered before He had someone to love Him!

The betrothed awaits His return and He comes and calls her to Him, for the season has come! She can now behold his countenance in secret places. Verse 14.

There are different ways that we think of "the secret places." Jesus is our Secret Place. We hide ourselves in Him. He covers us. But, we meet with Him in secret places. We may have actual physical places that we meet with Him in secret. We also have a secret spiritual place where we meet with Him.

What we do with Him in those secret places may be secret, as well. I could never begin to tell you what happens in the secret spiritual place in which I meet with the Lord. It is secret, private, personal and just for He and I. Everyone can have a secret place with Him.

Verse 15 recognizes that there are little foxes that come in and steal the sweet fruit. Those issues of life must be captured if we are to fully enjoy the fruit of this relationship. The little foxes are the sins of the flesh and soul that sour our walk with the Lord. They are also the temptations that the enemy uses to distract us from the pure love of our Lord.

Verse 16-17 say that they will be one another's until they are separated. [The mountain of Bether is literally "the mountain of separation."]

Chapter 3

In Chapter 3, she seeks Him but can't find Him. This relates to the Old Testament Church, the New Testament Church waiting for the rapture, and the individual believer looking in the wrong places and in the wrong ways to find Him. Sin and rebellion brought separation to the church. Call upon Him as the church would, He was not hearing because their hearts were far from Him.

As individual lovers of the Lord, we search in all the wrong places. We try all the religious stuff, all the formulas, all the spiritual exercises, and all the religious affectations. None bring us into His intimate presence! The only thing that works is to seek to love Him.

We are told to: "6 Seek ye the LORD while he may be found, call ye upon him while he is near: 7 Let the wicked forsake his way, and the unrighteous man his thoughts: and let him return unto the LORD, and he will have mercy upon him; and to our God, for he will abundantly pardon. 8 For my thoughts are not your thoughts, neither are your ways my ways, saith the LORD. 9 For as the heavens are higher than the earth, so are my ways higher than your ways, and my thoughts than your thoughts." Isaiah 55:7-9.

"9 And I say unto you, Ask, and it shall be given you; seek, and ye shall find; knock, and it shall be opened unto you. 10 For every one that asketh receiveth; and he that seeketh findeth; and to him that knocketh it shall be opened." Luke 11:9-10.

We know that David's heart ached for his desire to Love the Lord: "My soul thirsteth for God, for the living God: when shall I come and appear before God?" Psalm 42:2. Here in the Song, the Lover hungers for Him in the night.

She rises and seeks Him in the cold night. She asks the watchman who has no idea how to direct her. As Brother Lawrence asked his superiors and found that their techniques did not help him to find that deep intimate relationship with the Lord, so we ask others who do not have a clue. Our pastors, our friends, even our mentors may never have been in that secret place. They have religious answers but not personal experience. They may not even know that such a place exists. They may believe that their personal experience is all that there is. Remember, few have been there and only those who have been there can point the direction.

Once she finds Him, she holds on! Brother Lawrence found that after being in His presence, life and its attractions could distract him. He decided to hold on, forsaking other things. Put away all possible distractions. Just as "the cares and pleasures of life" can choke out the Word, so we are distracted by many things. How many marriages begin to self-destruct because one partner gets so busy with work or activities that there is no time for the relationship? Once you find Him, let go of everything else!

She brings her lover to her mother's house so that her family could know Him, too.

In verse 6, others question her beauty, referring to it as a smoke offering lifting to God. She quickly dismisses their praise of her and points to the King and His awesome glory!

There is nothing more attractive than one who is in love with Jesus. It can actually cause people to be attracted to us. We must always point back to our Husband. We must not begin to enjoy the fact that people are being drawn to us. Many real servants of God have been tripped up by seeking and enjoying the attention that their relationship with Jesus brings to them personally.

She describes the bed He has made for them as being guarded by mighty men of war and is a safe place for them. Jesus has created a way for us to come to Him. Our place with Him is guarded and safe. When we are in His presence none can touch us.

"1 He that dwelleth in the secret place of the most High shall abide under the shadow of the Almighty. 2 I will say of the LORD, He is my refuge and my fortress: my God; in him will I trust. 3 Surely he shall deliver thee from the snare of the fowler, and from the noisome pestilence. 4 He shall cover thee with his feathers, and under his wings shalt thou trust: his truth shall be thy shield and buckler. 5 Thou shalt not be afraid for the terror by night; nor for the arrow that flieth by day; 6 Nor for the pestilence that walketh in darkness; nor for the destruction that wasteth at noonday. 7 A thousand shall fall at thy side, and ten thousand at thy right hand; but it shall not come nigh thee. 8 Only with thine eyes shalt thou behold and see the reward of the wicked. 9 Because thou hast made the LORD, which is my refuge, even the most High, thy habitation; 10 There shall no evil befall thee, neither shall any plague come nigh thy dwelling." Psalm 91:1-10.

In verses 9-11, she speaks of the chariot that her lover has made for them to carry them to that bed. It is beautiful, expensive and plush with love.

Chapter 4

Chapter 4 begins again with the Lord singing praises for the Church and the individual believer. He finds no spot in her. Verse 7.

In verse 8, He invites her to come with Him.

He calls her his sister, his wife. Verse 9. God is a master of mixed metaphors. He represents Himself as male, but speaks of His mothering qualities. Jesus is our Father: "6 For unto us a child is born, unto us a son is given: and the government shall be upon his shoulder: and his name shall be called Wonderful, Counselor, Mighty God, Everlasting Father, Prince of Peace." Isaiah 9:6.

He is our friend. "Henceforth I call you not servants; for the servant knoweth not what his lord doeth: but I have called you friends; for all things that I have heard of my Father I have made known unto you." John 15:15.

He is called our brother: "15 For ye have not received the spirit of bondage again to fear; but ye have received the Spirit of adoption, whereby we cry, Abba, Father. 16 The Spirit itself beareth witness with our spirit, that we are the children of God: 17 And if children, then heirs; heirs of God, and joint-heirs with Christ; if so be that we suffer with him, that we may be also glorified together." Romans 8:15-17.

He is our brother, but is also our husband: "I will greatly rejoice in the LORD, my soul shall be joyful in my God; for he hath clothed me with the garments of salvation, he hath covered me with the robe of righteousness, as a bridegroom decketh himself with ornaments, and as a bride adorneth herself with her jewels." Isaiah 61:10.

"And there came unto me one of the seven angels which had the seven vials full of the seven last plagues, and talked with me, saying, Come hither, I will show thee the bride, the Lamb's wife." Revelation 21:9.

So, the lover is His sister, and she is His wife. This is a mixed metaphor, but if you pursue that thought, how much closer, how much more related could one be than to be sister *and* wife? By blood, and by marriage we are made one with the Lord! We share the same Father.

In verse 12, He says she is like a garden locked. She is precious and beautiful, but unavailable. Her gates are locked. We may say we love Him, but we often make ourselves unavailable. We want Him, but we do not want to let Him come in and have all of us. If we keep the gates locked, we will never know the passion of allowing Him to have His way with us.

Even in marriage, people withhold themselves from one another. In our relationship with God, there are places we do not permit Him to go. There are things that we withhold from Him. Anything we withhold from the Lord is an idol. Anything we withhold, we love more than Him!

In verse 16, she decides to let Him in for passionate intimacy. She makes herself available to Him. Take me, Lord! All of me! Everything I am, everything I have! My very life, my very breath! It is all yours! You created it! You redeemed it! You own it! Take me Lord!!

Chapter 5

Chapter 5 opens with the Lord saying that He has come in to His lover and delighted in her. He then encourages us and lets us know that we, too, may partake of this intimate, passionate, unbridled love with Him!

After the honeymoon, the inevitable happens: He calls to her and she does not let Him in. She is tired and doesn't jump at His call. He withdraws. She excuses herself by saying that she has already settled down and it would be too much trouble to get up and let Him in. So we do to the Lord, even after we have experienced His intimate loving touch. The cares and pleasures of life distract us. Laziness or fatigue distracts us. If we don't FEEL like it, we don't go to Him.

My first appointment every day is with the Lord at 4:30 a.m. Many a morning He calls and beckons to me to get up and come and walk with Him. In the past, there were days that I balk at even that great an invitation! He withdrew. Now, no matter how I FEEL, if He calls, I go!

His lover, now convicted and filled with desire, gets up to let Him in, but it is too late. He has withdrawn. Now frantic, she runs all over looking for Him. Because of the way she is acting and the fact that she is out at such an hour, the night guards take her for a sinner and beat her, administering a little street justice. When we spurn the Lord and go our own way, we come out from under His covering and anointing. We make ourselves open to the Evil One to beat up on us.

She asks others to intercede for her that she might find Him. Verse 8.

Some who are asked to intercede for her scorn her and suggest that she shouldn't care so much that she has lost that intimacy with Him. Verse 9. Those who do not understand, who have never tasted of His delights, think it unimportant that we have lost that closeness. They do not know that His kiss is the very breath of life to us who have experienced intimacy with Him. They think nothing of the things of life that truly interfere with our relationship with Him.

She responds again by extolling and exalting Him and speaking of His delights. Even though she has allowed separation, she knows the truth!

In verse 16, she ends her current exultation and calls Him her beloved and her friend. He is not only our lover, He is our friend. (John 15:15)

48

Now they want to know where they can find Him, too. She responds that He has gone to His gardens, His quiet place.

Having been frantic to find Him, she now begins to speak in faith: "I am my beloved's and He is mine." When we can't see or feel Him, we need to take His presence by faith. We need to be secure that He really does love us and that we are secure in that love, no matter what we feel or see. ("For we walk by faith and not by sight." 2 Corinthians 5:7) The feeling of His passion is wonderful! Yet, even when we can't feel the passion, we need to KNOW the reality and rest in it. Passions ebb and flow. Even in the most passionate marriage, there are cooler times.

In verses 4-10, He returns to her. He blesses her. He has missed her! In verse 9, He suggests that there is none like her. There are many others (verse 8) but they do not compare!

In reality, He can say that honestly to each one of us. The love He has for me is special and unique. No one else can have it. The love He has for you is equally unique and equally intimate, special and intense. When He is with me, there is no other!

While they were apart, He watched over her to see how she would develop. Verse 11.

In her desire, she suddenly found herself back with her lover in a swift chariot. Verse 12. He came to her and swooped her up into His chariot. [Elijah was also taken up into the chariot of God.] Their breech is healed. They are united and one.

In verse 13, she is called by another title; O Shulammite. As best as we can understand, this means that she is now "of Solomon", as Christians are "of Christ."

Now the world calls to her "return, return, that we may look upon you." The world and Satan do not want us to give ourselves totally to the Lord; they call, they plead, they entice. The bride is seen as one dancing before two armies. We hang between the world and the Kingdom of God, being drawn in both directions. Intellectually there is no contest. Emotionally the battle rages between the spirit and the flesh.

Chapter 7

He entices her by singing His love songs over her and exalting her. Verses 1-9. Worship is lovemaking. We speak lovingly to our Lord and He speaks lovingly to us. Worship is conversation. Worship is a two-way experience. Worship is communion. Worship is intercourse. If your worship is only one way, you are missing out!

This is intimate worship. As elsewhere, He rejoices in her breasts!

Verse 4 refers to the fish pools of Heshbon. This is a very fertile place. Bath-Rabbim means Daughter of Multitudes.

In verses 10-13, she now declares her willingness and desire to go all the way with Him and give Him everything.

Chapter 8

She now desires the fullest love possible. In the mixed metaphor, He has called her "My sister, my bride." Now, she mixes a metaphor and expresses a desire for Him to be her brother and her husband. She wants that total, intense, oneness with Him.

In verse 5, the world takes note of her as she is now clearly with the Lord. She is recognized as His.

In verse 5b, the Lord announces that He created her for this purpose. Psalm 139:13 tells us that God knitted us together in the womb. I know that I was created to worship Him!

In verse 6, she asks Him to confirm forever that she will always be in Him and asks for a visible seal of this everlasting bond.

"Behold, I have graven thee upon the palms of my hands; thy walls are continually before me." Isaiah 49:16.

"13 In whom ye also trusted, after that ye heard the word of truth, the gospel of your salvation: in whom also after that ye believed, ye were sealed with that holy Spirit of promise, 14 Which is the earnest of our inheritance until the redemption of the purchased possession, unto the praise of his glory." Ephesians

1:13-14. "And grieve not the holy Spirit of God, whereby ye are sealed unto the day of redemption." Ephesians 4:30.

She pleads that the strength of love is worthy of this. It is stronger than death. It dislikes anything that might draw it away. It is a consuming fire!

"38 For I am persuaded, that neither death, nor life, nor angels, nor principalities, nor powers, nor things present, nor things to come, 39 Nor height, nor depth, nor any other creature, shall be able to separate us from the love of God, which is in Christ Jesus our Lord." Romans 8:38-39.

There is not a thing in the world that would entice me to trade the Love of the Lord!

Now the husband and wife talk of family affairs. The scholars suggest that here the older sister is the Jewish church speaking of the Christian Church which, at the time of this writing had not yet experienced the attraction of the Lord. The Lord suggests that He will find a way to build her into the temple.

Other scholars suggest that verses 8 and 9 refer to the spouse looking back at her husband, elder brother watching over her when she was young and wayward. Verse 10, then, would be an expression of her growing up, maturing, and finding favor with the Lord.

Verses 11-12 talk of the church as the vineyard. It is supposed to bear fruit. To each is given talents. Each of us is responsible to use our giftings to bring an increase proportionate to the gift to the gift that we have been given. We are to do the best we can with what we have. (See Matthew 25:14-30.)

In Verse 13, the Bride asks her Husband to keep their communication open as He works in the garden. Here again some take this as the request of the Jewish Church to the Lord to keep their communication open during the period of the Gentiles. And verse 14 is her request that her Husband return for her quickly.

The book ends abruptly, leaving us dissatisfied and incomplete. No matter how great our communion with the Lord, He has yet to return for us. He is with us, but He is not here. And:

"1 For we know that if our earthly house of this tabernacle

51

were dissolved, we have a building of God, an house not made with hands, eternal in the heavens. 2 For in this we groan, earnestly desiring to be clothed upon with our house which is from heaven: 3 If so be that being clothed we shall not be found naked. 4 For we that are in this tabernacle do groan, being burdened: not for that we would be unclothed, but clothed upon, that mortality might be swallowed up of life. 5 Now he that hath wrought us for the selfsame thing is God, who also hath given unto us the earnest of the Spirit. 6 Therefore we are always confident, knowing that, whilst we are at home in the body, we are absent from the Lord: 7 (For we walk by faith, not by sight:) 8 We are confident, I say, and willing rather to be absent from the body, and to be present with the Lord. 9 Wherefore we labour, that, whether present or absent, we may be accepted of him." 2 Corinthians 5:1-9.

Commentary

It does not matter whether you are male or female. Jesus is your Husband and wants to be intimate with you. How secure are you in Him? How vulnerable are you to Him? How far in are you willing to allow Him to come? How passionate are you willing to be with Him?

You set the pace. You set the limits. You choose the level of desire.

CHAPTER SIX

THE BRIDE

"I will greatly rejoice in the LORD, my soul shall be joyful in my God; for he hath clothed me with the garments of salvation, he hath covered me with the robe of righteousness, as a bridegroom decketh himself with ornaments, and as a bride adorneth herself with her jewels." Isaiah 61:10.

"For as a young man marrieth a virgin, so shall thy sons marry thee: and as the bridegroom rejoiceth over the bride, so shall thy God rejoice over thee." Isaiah 62:5.

"4 Fear not; for thou shalt not be ashamed: neither be thou confounded; for thou shalt not be put to shame: for thou shalt forget the shame of thy youth, and shalt not remember the reproach of thy widowhood any more. 5 For thy Maker is thine husband; the LORD of hosts is his name; and thy Redeemer the Holy One of Israel; The God of the whole earth shall he be called. 6 For the LORD hath called thee as a woman forsaken and grieved in spirit, and a wife of youth, when thou wast refused, saith thy God." Isaiah 54:4-6.

"10 Hearken, O daughter, and consider, and incline thine ear; forget also thine own people, and thy father's house; 11 So shall the king greatly desire thy beauty: for he is thy Lord; and worship thou him." [Bow yourself down to Him.] Psalm 45:10-11.

The church is the Bride of Christ. The marriage will take place when He comes to rapture the church. We will be taken to the marriage feast of the Lamb.

As a believer, you are individually the Bride of Christ. You became His Bride on the day you got saved. It does not matter if you are male or female. Women have little problem with this concept. They know that when they are widowed, Jesus becomes their Husband. He will cover them, protect them, and meet their needs.

Men, too!

Men on the other hand are not trained to be in the submissive role. Many men are insecure in their sexuality or their sexual role. The thought of playing the part of the submissive wife, bowing herself down to her husband is offensive to them. They would rather make coarse jokes, talk sports, or shoot some hoops. The Lord would like to do all of those things with them [except the coarse jesting!]. However, there are others like John the beloved, who was at peace with an open physical display of affection with Jesus.

Those men will enter into an incredible experience of intimacy that others will never know. You can laugh with Him, cry with Him, kiss Him, sing to Him and receive the same from Him! You are His Bride! In heaven, sex and gender are NOT an issue! In Christ there is neither male or female. (Galatians 3:28) In Heaven we are neither married to one another or given in marriage. (Matthew 22:30)

What kind of Bride are you?

You will either be a loving bride or an unfaithful wife. You will enjoy intimacy with Him or you will miss out on the purpose of your salvation. You will either be the virtuous wife of Proverbs 31 fame, or you will be rebellious, nagging, or adulterous.

When I married thirty-two years ago, I was a terrible husband and my wife did not meet my needs. Life was miserable and unfulfilling. We were unhappy in our union. Now, we are passionately in love with one another. We are fulfilled and blessed.

To a large degree, that came about as we each grew closer to the Lord. The more I love Jesus, the better able I am to love my wife. The closer we grow to the Lord, the closer we grow to one another. In addition, we tried to learn how to be good spouses. We honored one another. We wooed one another. We practiced our sexuality together. We practiced our spirituality together. We learned to enjoy our similarities and our differences.

Many spouses don't try. They expect their partner to do all the relationship work and to learn what makes a marriage work. Many a Christian approaches the marriage bed with the Lamb in the same fashion. They expect the Lord to do all the work, to make all the changes, to put up with all their willfulness and selfish demanding.

A good wife will prepare herself for her husband. She will make herself attractive and desirable. She will try to learn what is pleasing to her husband.

You do Commands

When we read that we are a new creation in Christ, we expect that Jesus is going to make us different all by Himself. The fact that this does not happen automatically leads many to question the Word, some to question their salvation, and others to come to believe that Jesus loves others but not them. Why doesn't anyone tell us that we need to grow in Him? We are to be transformed into the image of the Son. That is a process. We are to grow into the fullness of the measure of the stature of Christ. That is a process. We are to be transformed by the renewal of the mind. The Greek word for "transformed" is *metamorphismo,* and a metamorphosis is clearly a process. It happens by getting our head in agreement with God and out of agreement with the world.

[TO THE DEGREE YOU AGREE WITH GOD, THE POWER OF GOD IS MANIFEST IN YOUR LIFE. TO THE DEGREE YOU DISAGREE WITH GOD, THE POWER OF GOD IS DIMINISHED IN YOUR LIFE.]

There are a lot of "you do" commands in the Word. If we study to show ourselves approved, we will see what our Husband requires us to do. If we do what He commands us to do, He will do what He promises to do in us. [See Joshua 1:6-9]

55

Love Decides

The quality of love you have for the Lord will decide what kind of a bride you will be. It will also decide how much access you have to the marriage bed. Love will desire to be the best and do the best for the Lord. Lust will be demanding that He perform for you.

Wherever He goes, you will follow. Whatever He wants, you will do. You will do it when He asks. You will seek to know His will and you will willingly do it, no matter what it costs.

CHAPTER SEVEN

THE REAL GOD

When two people marry, they seldom marry the person they believe they are marrying. We marry an image. That image is made up of what we hope our spouse will be and the image that our spouse has presented to us during courtship. As time goes on, we begin to realize that what we got was not what we thought we had. The distance between our imaginary spouse and the reality of whom and what our spouse really is, represents the level of our fulfillment or dissatisfaction with our marriage. In order to bring satisfaction and fulfillment, we either have to accept our spouse for who he or she *really* is, or our spouse needs to become what we want him or her to be. [FAT CHANCE!!!!!!!]

Anthropomorphic god

We do the same thing with God. Our God is anthropomorphic. That is, we create an image of God out of our life experience and out of our desire. Life has given us a definition for the word "Father." God calls himself "Father." Our meaning for that word now describes for us what God is. We may see Him as:

> Mean and cruel.
> Unforgiving.
> Unfair and selective.
> Absent.
> Weak and insipid.
> Not providing.

Allowing and tolerating anything; permissive.

Extremely controlling.

Not loving, or saying he loves us but never demonstrating it.

Untrustworthy, not keeping his promises.

In today's world, more than likely, the god of our creation is seen as absent and totally accepting. We latch onto theologies like "Once saved, always saved" which we *interpret* to mean that as long as we have prayed "the prayer of salvation" we can do ANYTHING and still be saved. Another pet theology is "Ultimate reconciliation." This one says that we will just go through a brief time of punishment to chastise us for our sin and then we will all be reconciled to God. It is unacceptable to believe that our god would send anyone to Hell forever! We hear people say, on many issues, "*My god* would never do that!"

Will the REAL God please stand up.

We are afraid to find out who God really is. We lie about Him. We theologize Him into submission to our desire. "30 For we know him that hath said, Vengeance belongeth unto me, I will recompense, saith the Lord. And again, The Lord shall judge his people. 31 It is a fearful thing to fall into the hands of the living God." Hebrews 10:30-31.

Romans 3:4 tells us to let God be true though every man be a liar. God wants us to go to Him to find out who He really is. The only way to be really happy with God is to accept Him for who He really is. He is King, Judge, Savior, and Eternal God. He shows wrath, anger, mercy, love, kindness, and He dishes out strong discipline on those He loves.

The Real God Deals with His Children!

"1 Wherefore seeing we also are compassed about with so great a cloud of witnesses, let us lay aside every weight, and the sin which doth so easily beset us, and let us run with patience the race that is set before us, 2 Looking unto Jesus the author and finisher of our faith; who for the joy that was set before him endured the cross, despising the shame, and is set down at the right hand of the throne of God. 3 For consider him that endured such contradiction of sinners against himself, lest ye be wearied and faint in your minds. 4 Ye have not yet resisted unto blood, striving against sin. 5 And ye have forgotten the exhortation which speaketh unto you as unto children, My son, despise not thou the chastening of the Lord, nor faint when thou art rebuked of him: 6 For whom the Lord loveth he chasteneth, and scourgeth every son whom he receiveth. 7 If ye endure chastening, God dealeth with you as with sons; for what son is he whom the father hasteneth not? 8 But if ye be without chastisement, whereof all are partakers, then are ye bastards, and not sons. 9 Furthermore we have had fathers of our flesh which corrected us, and we gave them reverence: shall we not much rather be in subjection unto the Father of spirits, and live? 10 For they verily for a few days chastened us after their own pleasure; but he for our profit, that we might be partakers of his holiness. 11 Now no chastening for the present seemeth to be joyous, but grievous: nevertheless afterward it yieldeth the peaceable fruit of righteousness unto them which are exercised thereby. 12 Wherefore lift up the hands which hang down, and the feeble knees; 13 And make straight paths for your feet, lest that which is lame be turned out of the way; but let it rather be healed." Hebrews 12:1-13.

The real God will judge His people and the people of the world. "26 For if we sin willfully after that we have received the knowledge of the truth, there remaineth no more sacrifice for sins, 27 But a certain fearful looking for of judgment and fiery indignation, which shall devour the adversaries." Hebrews 10:26-27.

The Real God Offends Our Sensitivities

For some, the thought of being a Lover of God, or more descriptively, God's Lover, is as totally offensive as the judgment of God and His demand for obedience are to others.

Clichés Protect Us

We have all kinds of clichés about God:

God is a gentleman. He would never embarrass you.
   Tell that to David dancing in His underwear!

God will never let anything bad ever happen to you, if you have faith.
   Tell that to Paul. (Acts 9:16) (2 Corinthians 11:22-29)

God will never allow sickness.
   Tell that to Lazarus. "When Jesus heard that {Lazarus was sick}, he said, This sickness is not unto death, but for the glory of God, that the Son of God might be glorified thereby." John 11:4.

God wants you to be happy, so go ahead and ......
   Show me the Biblical doctrine of happiness! Show me God saying sin is acceptable if it makes you happy!

God will never expose your sin to others.
   Tell that to Ananias and Sappira. (Acts 5:1-11) Tell that to the prophets.

God doesn't require the tithe anymore.
   "6 For I am the LORD, I change not; therefore ye sons of Jacob are not consumed... 8 Will a man rob God? Yet ye have robbed me. But ye say, Wherein have we robbed thee? In tithes and offerings. 9 Ye are cursed with a curse: for ye have robbed me, even this whole nation. 10 Bring ye all the tithes into the storehouse, that there may be meat in mine house, and prove me now herewith, saith the LORD of hosts, if I will not open you the windows of heaven, and pour you out a blessing, that there shall not be room enough to receive it." Malachi 3:6,8-10.

Your Anthropomorphic God is an Idol

We could go on forever. The point is that you will never have intimacy with God until you are willing to experience Him as He really is. When we create a god of our own liking we are practicing idolatry!

"1 And when the people saw that Moses delayed to come down out of the mount, the people gathered themselves together unto Aaron, and said unto him, Up, make us gods, which shall go before us; for as for this Moses, the man that brought us up out of the land of Egypt, we wot not what is become of him. 2 And Aaron said unto them, Break off the golden earrings, which are in the ears of your wives, of your sons, and of your daughters, and bring them unto me. 3 And all the people brake off the golden earrings which were in their ears, and brought them unto Aaron. 4 And he received them at their hand, and fashioned it with a graving tool, after he had made it a molten calf: and they said, These be thy gods, O Israel, which brought thee up out of the land of Egypt. 5 And when Aaron saw it, he built an altar before it; and Aaron made proclamation, and said, Tomorrow is a feast to the LORD. 6 And they rose up early on the morrow, and offered burnt offerings, and brought peace offerings; and the people sat down to eat and to drink, and rose up to play." Exodus 32:1-6.

"1 Moreover, brethren, I would not that ye should be ignorant, how that all our fathers were under the cloud, and all passed through the sea; 2 And were all baptized unto Moses in the cloud and in the sea; 3 And did all eat the same spiritual meat; 4 And did all drink the same spiritual drink: for they drank of that spiritual Rock that followed them: and that Rock was Christ. 5 But with many of them God was not well pleased: for they were overthrown in the wilderness. 6 Now these things were our examples, to the intent we should not lust after evil things, as they also lusted. 7 Neither be ye idolaters, as were some of them; as it is written, The people sat down to eat and drink, and rose up to play. 8 Neither let us commit fornication, as some of them committed, and fell in one day three and twenty thousand. 9 Neither let us tempt Christ, as some of them also tempted, and were destroyed of serpents. 10 Neither murmur ye, as some of them also murmured, and were destroyed of the destroyer. 11 Now all these things happened unto them for ensamples: and they are written for our admonition, upon whom the ends of the world are come. 12 Wherefore let him that thinketh he standeth take heed lest he fall. 13 There hath no temptation taken you but such as is common to man: but God is faithful, who will not suffer you to be tempted above that ye are able; but will with the temptation also make a way to escape, that ye may be able to bear it." 1 Corinthians 10:1-13.

There is only One God. He alone defines the rules. He speaks for Himself. He has revealed Himself in His Word and in His Names, and in His Son. If we want to be a lover of God, we need to TOTALLY submit to Him! We need to totally accept ALL of Him! We need to accept our place and our purpose. We need to accept reality.

"But now, O LORD, thou art our father; we are the clay, and thou our potter; and we all are the work of thy hand." Isaiah 64:8.

"20 Nay but, O man, who art thou that repliest against God? Shall the thing formed say to him that formed it, Why hast thou made me thus? 21 Hath not the potter power over the clay, of the same lump to make one vessel unto honour, and another unto dishonour?" Romans 9:20-21.

What Does it Mean to Love Him?

`We have already seen that there are three Greek words in the Bible which are translated "love." If you add to this variety of meanings our definitions based on our life experience, we can see how hard it is to understand what it means to love God.

David says: "...As the hart panteth after the water brooks, so panteth my soul after thee, O God." Psalm 42:1b. What does he mean? Is he poetically saying that he would like a deeper relationship with God or is he saying that his insides hurt with longing for an intimate love relationship with God?

Most people read the Word without ever understanding what it is really saying.

Lord I Want to Know YOU!

O Lord, I want to know you. I am sick of hearing what people say about You. I want You! Just as You are! Please open Your Word to me. Please reveal Your Names to me. Please show me who You are. I give myself to You. Do with me WHATEVER You want. Make me whatever You want me to be. Let's get REAL! I'm sick of the sham! I want TRUTH!

CHAPTER EIGHT

I SAID IT WAS *MY* CHURCH!

"1 I therefore, the prisoner of the Lord, beseech you that ye walk worthy of the vocation wherewith ye are called, 2 With all lowliness and meekness, with longsuffering, forbearing one another in love; 3 Endeavouring to keep the unity of the Spirit in the bond of peace. 4 *There is* one body, and one Spirit, even as ye are called in one hope of your calling; 5 One Lord, one faith, one baptism, 6 One God and Father of all, who *is* above all, and through all, and in you all." Ephesians 4:1-6.

"...Christ is the head of the church: and he is the saviour of the body." Ephesians 5:23b.

One of the pieces of information that God downloaded into me when I got saved was about the Body of Christ. God showed me the Body as it was supposed to be: an army, under His command, standing together, worshipping together, and fighting against a common enemy. He gave me a vision of Christians standing arm in arm. He told me that it was my job to call the Body to unity.

I figured, "No problem! If we all love the Lord and recognize the price He paid to save us, we would all stand in unity and obey His command!" How wrong I was. At that time, I knew nothing about the Body of Christ! When I found out the reality, I was confused, upset, angry, and perplexed! Sure we have denominational differences. We all like different flavors of ice cream. We all like different styles of music. But, we were never intended to have our own Kingdom, which we would share with no one else.

One night while I was still in seminary, I went to a service of ordination for a friend from school. He belonged to a different denomination, but I knew he loved the Lord. He was to be permitted to minister Communion for the first time at this service. What an honor it would be to receive Communion from my brother in Christ.

Before the service began, he came to me and explained that I would not be permitted to receive Communion that night. Even though he knew me, his denomination had not had the opportunity to examine me and approve me to receive! I had never heard of "Closed" or "Close" Communion before. I was incredulous!

We not only have denominations, we have varieties of the same denominations. There are several kinds of Catholics, several kinds of Lutherans, Presbyterians, Methodists, etc. We not only have bunches of similar denominations, we have individual churches who relate to, and submit to NO ONE! Some of those denominations and some of those individual churches actually believe that only their members will be saved, because salvation comes through them!

I think my biggest shock, though, came when I realized that missionaries not only did not support one another, they actually fought over territory! There have been reports of missionaries actually burning down the mission stations of competitors!

I Counted Them In

I was determined to do what the Lord told me. I prayed for unity in the Body. I made calls, I knocked on church doors, and I invited pastors. More often than not, doors were closed, calls refused, invitations turned down. When I shared my vision with others who would listen, they would explain to me why it would not work. After all, "You know how THEY are."

A poet said it well:

"They drew a circle and included me out.

I drew a circle and included them in."

I determined that I would include in my circle anyone who believed in salvation by grace through faith alone, the deity of Christ, the atoning Blood of the Lamb, and the Word of God. I didn't care a whole lot about what other odd things they might believe. Whether they liked it or not, by the Blood of the Lamb, I was their brother!

The True Body

After thirty-six years of trying, sometimes harder than others, I now realize that the true Body is not restricted by denominations or pastoral attitudes. The body of Christ is found wherever an individual loves Him! There are believers in all denominations. There are some believers who are still in abominations, because they haven't yet seen the heresy of the group they are in.

God is not waiting for denominations. He isn't waiting for pastors. They are too busy building their kingdoms and fighting for their place within those kingdoms. They are not interested in God's Kingdom or God's Church.

The Name on the Door

The name on the door where you worship means little to God. The Name on your heart means everything! Where is your allegiance? To whom are you committed? For what will you give your life?

True Believers Include One Another In

True believers recognize the Spirit of God wherever they see it. They do not care where you worship. They just care that you do worship! True believers LOVE one another as Christ loved us! True believers know that this is how the world will come to recognize who the Lord is! It was Jesus' prayer:

"20 Neither pray I for these alone, but for them also which shall believe on me through their word; 21 That they all may be one; as thou, Father, art in me, and I in thee, that they also may be one in us: that the world may believe that thou hast sent me. ...23 I in them, and thou in me, that they may be made perfect in one; and that the world may know that thou hast sent me, and hast loved them, as thou hast loved me." John 17:20-21, 23.

True believers follow the command of the Lord: "34 A new commandment I give unto you, That ye love one another; as I have loved you, that ye also love one another. 35 By this shall all men know that ye are my disciples, if ye have love one to another." John 13:34-35.

CHAPTER NINE

THE COST - PART ONE

Eternal life is a free gift of grace received by faith. It cannot be earned or deserved. It cannot be repaid after you attain it. However, abiding in Christ and growing in the Lord will require everything that you are and have!

I frequently accuse the body of Christ of practicing "bait and switch" tactics. We promise that if they accept Jesus as their Savior, everything will be wonderful. We don't tell them about spiritual warfare, dying to self, and abandoning everything for the cause. Salvation is free, but it will cost you your very life!

His Plan for You

God's plan is to groom us to love Him and serve Him. His personal plan for us is first our salvation and then our sanctification. He desires us to grow into the fullness of the measure of the stature of the manhood of Christ. (Ephesians 4:13) He wants us to become a new creature in Christ. (2 Corinthians 5:17) He wants us to be transformed by the renewal of our mind. (Romans 12:2) He wants us to put to death the things of the flesh and put on the things of the spirit. (Colossians 3:5-9)

He wants us saved, clean, holy, righteous, pure and dead to self so that our love may be pure and true. He wants us totally available to Him, without reservation. He does not want to share us with anyone or anything.

Salvation

If you are reading this, I hope that salvation already belongs to you. Without it, it is impossible to see God. Salvation is a free gift of grace, received by faith, it is not of works. (Ephesians 2:8-9) Through salvation we are adopted as children of God. (Romans 8:15-17) As children of God, we have direct access to the Father. (Hebrews 4:16) We do not need to fear rejection, because we have already been accepted through Jesus' sacrifice. (1 John 4:18)

Sanctification

Sanctification is a different story. Sanctification is a process that brings us into obedience to Christ. Sanctification brings us into the favor of God. Imagine three children coming before their father. All are loved, cared for, and provided for. All have access to their father.

Two of the three love their parents and are obedient. They do not cause trouble in the house. They do not bring shame to the family name. They obey their parents and the law. The third is rebellious, demanding, independent, quarrelsome and disrespectful. Would you expect the latter to be greeted the same as the first two? Would you expect the same favor and grace for the third as for the first two? Of course not!

Sanctification gets rid of the sins of the flesh and brings us into real Lordship.

Lordship means:

> Whatever you want, Lord.
> Whenever you want it, Lord.
> Wherever you want it, Lord.
> No matter how much it costs me.

Jesus asked, "Why do you call me Lord, Lord and not do what I say?" Luke 6:46.

Sanctification brings us into favor with the Lord.

One Left

There is also a difference between the two obedient children. They both love and obey, but one desires to be just like his father. He desires to honor his father with his very life. He loves his father passionately and desires to be with him, talk with him, and listen to him.

It is almost impossible for a parent to be totally impartial. We are all equally loved, but we do not all share the same place of intimacy or favor.

Sanctification and Dying to Self are Processes

While we may wish to get the sanctification process over quickly, this depth of love does not just happen. It is a painful process. It cannot be approached academically, it has to be experienced. Growth can't be learned in a classroom. Dying to self doesn't occur on the chalkboard. Pressure brings things to the surface. The fire brings cleansing. Dying to self is painful.

Paul's Example

Childhood and adolescence are painful. There are many tears, rejections and losses. To grow in the Lord requires us to die to self and live to the Spirit. Paul offers us a beautiful example of one dying to self. Paul was a man of stature. He was a Roman citizen. He had come from wealth. He was trained as a Pharisee, well educated and groomed for leadership. His use of the Greek language shows that he had an advanced intellect. His presentations in the letters to the Romans and Hebrews show a keen understanding of theology. He had a lot going for him.

Yet, Paul died to self. He says:

"I am crucified with Christ: nevertheless I live; yet not I, but Christ liveth in me: and the life which I now live in the flesh I live by the faith of the Son of God, who loved me, and gave himself for me." Galatians 2:20.

"7 But what things were gain to me, those I counted loss for Christ. 8 Yea doubtless, and I count all things but loss for the excellency of the knowledge of Christ Jesus my Lord: for whom I have suffered the loss of all things, and do count them but dung, that I may win Christ, 9 And be found in him, not having mine own righteousness, which is of the law, but that which is through the faith of Christ, the righteousness which is of God by faith:" Philippians 3:7-9.

"Not that we are sufficient of ourselves to think any thing as · of ourselves; but our sufficiency is of God;" 2 Corinthians 3:5.

"But we have this treasure in earthen vessels, that the excellency of the power may be of God, and not of us." 2 Corinthians 4:7.

"To whom God would make known what is the riches of the glory of this mystery among the Gentiles; which is Christ in you, the hope of glory:" Colossians 1:27.

"21 For to me to live *is* Christ, and to die *is* gain. 22 But if I live in the flesh, this *is* the fruit of my labour: yet what I shall choose I wot not. 23 For I am in a strait betwixt two, having a desire to depart, and to be with Christ; which is far better: 24 Nevertheless to abide in the flesh *is* more needful for you. 25 And having this confidence, I know that I shall abide and continue with you all for your furtherance and joy of faith; 26 That your rejoicing may be more abundant in Jesus Christ for me by my coming to you again." Philippians 1:21-26.

Count the Cost

In order for Paul to have gotten to this place, he had to die to self. Since he was so strong a human being to begin, dying was hard and costly. The stronger our temperament, our willpower, our intestinal fortitude, the harder we die. Paul paid a high price for sanctification and death of the flesh:

"23 Are they ministers of Christ? (I speak as a fool) I am more; in labours more abundant, in stripes above measure, in prisons more frequent, in deaths oft. 24 Of the Jews five times received I forty stripes save one. 25 Thrice was I beaten with rods, once was I stoned, thrice I suffered shipwreck, a night and a day I have been in the deep; 26 In journeyings often, in perils of waters, in perils of robbers, in perils by mine own countrymen, in perils by the heathen, in perils in the city, in perils in the wilderness, in perils in the sea, in perils among false brethren; 27 In weariness and painfulness, in watchings often, in hunger and thirst, in fastings often, in cold and nakedness. 28 Beside those things that are without, that which cometh upon me daily, the care of all the churches. 29 Who is weak, and I am not weak? who is offended, and I burn not? 30 If I must needs glory, I will glory of the things which concern mine infirmities." 2 Corinthians 11:23-30.

Paul lost his hope of promotion in the Jewish church system. He left his bright future in church politics only to be rejected by many of the Christian believers. Many in the church did not trust him. In the world, he was cold, hungry, shipwrecked, beaten, arrested and harassed by Jews and Christians alike. He suffered hunger and want. At times, he had to work at making tents just to support himself and his ministry.

Paul paid a great price to die to self so that he could love and trust the Lord. Paul's life became nothing. Jesus became everything!

No, Paul did not miss it because he didn't have enough faith! Paul found it! This was Jesus' Gospel!

"26 If any man come to me, and hate not his father, and mother, and wife, and children, and brethren, and sisters, yea, and his own life also, he cannot be my disciple. 27 And whosoever doth not bear his cross, and come after me, cannot be my disciple. 28 For which of you, intending to build a tower, sitteth not down first, and counteth the cost, whether he have sufficient to finish it? 29 Lest haply, after he hath laid the foundation, and is not able to finish it, all that behold it begin to mock him, 30 Saying, This man began to build, and was not able to finish. 31 Or what king, going to make war against another king, sitteth not down first, and consulteth whether he be able with ten thousand to meet him that cometh against him with twenty thousand? 32 Or else, while the other is yet a great way off, he sendeth an ambassage, and desireth conditions of peace." Luke 14:26-32.

Paul understood this from the time of his salvation. But the Lord said unto him, "15...for he is a chosen vessel unto me, to bear my name before the Gentiles, and kings, and the children of Israel: 16 For I will show him how great things he must suffer for my name's sake." Acts 9:15b-16.

The Baptism of Fire

"I indeed baptize you with water unto repentance: but he that cometh after me is mightier than I, whose shoes I am not worthy to bear: he shall baptize you with the Holy Ghost, and with fire:" Matthew 3:11.

This baptism of fire, or suffering is required if we want to go further into the Lord and die to self. Elijah and Elisha suffered it. The Israelites experienced it:

14....the LORD thy God, which brought thee forth out of the land of Egypt, from the house of bondage; 15 Who led thee through that great and terrible wilderness, *wherein were* fiery serpents, and scorpions, and drought, where *there was* no water; who brought thee forth water out of the rock of flint; 16 Who fed thee in the wilderness with manna, which thy fathers knew not, that he might humble thee, and that he might prove thee, to do thee good at thy latter end;" Deuteronomy 8:14b-16.

Proverbs talks about it: "The fining pot *is* for silver, and the furnace for gold: but the LORD trieth the hearts." Proverbs 17:3.

The New Testament tells us to expect it: "6 Wherein ye greatly rejoice, though now for a season, if need be, ye are in heaviness through manifold temptations: 7 That the trial of your faith, being much more precious than of gold that perisheth, though it be tried with fire, might be found unto praise and honour and glory at the appearing of Jesus Christ:" 1 Peter 1:6-7.

"4 Ye have not yet resisted unto blood, striving against sin. 5 And ye have forgotten the exhortation which speaketh unto you as unto children, My son, despise not thou the chastening of the Lord, nor faint when thou art rebuked of him: 6 For whom the Lord loveth he chasteneth, and scourgeth every son whom he receiveth. 7 If ye endure chastening, God dealeth with you as with sons; for what son is he whom the father chasteneth not? 8 But if ye be without chastisement, whereof all are partakers, then are ye bastards, and not sons. 9 Furthermore we have had fathers of our flesh which corrected *us*, and we gave *them* reverence: shall we not much rather be in subjection unto the Father of spirits, and live? 10 For they verily for a few days chastened *us* after their own pleasure; but he for *our* profit, that *we* might be partakers of his holiness. 11 Now no chastening for the present seemeth to be joyous, but grievous: nevertheless afterward it yieldeth the peaceable fruit of righteousness unto them which are exercised thereby. 12 Wherefore lift up the hands which hang down, and the feeble knees; 13 And make straight paths for your feet, lest that which is lame be turned out of the way; but let it rather be healed." Hebrews 12:4-13.

"19 As many as I love, I rebuke and chasten: be zealous therefore, and repent. 20 Behold, I stand at the door, and knock: if any man hear my voice, and open the door, I will come in to him, and will sup with him, and he with me. 21 To him that overcometh will I grant to sit with me in my throne, even as I also overcame, and am set down with my Father in his throne. 22 He that hath an ear, let him hear what the Spirit saith unto the churches." Revelation 3:19-22.

How far are you willing to go? You may stop at any time.

We Have to Mention Job

The entire Book of Job is an example of the process. Job also shows us what our friends will tell us as we are going through the process. Believe me, friends will think that you have hidden sin in your life and that surely God has turned His back on you! To the contrary, He will show you His face! They will question your faith. They will be certain that you are suffering because you are out of the will of God. They will not understand, because they have never been there. They will not understand because your experience doesn't fit their theology. *Their* God would NEVER do such a thing! They don't want *their* God to ever do that to them. They will also never know God, as you will!

Along the way, it can get scary. You will wonder what is becoming of you. You will wonder just how great the price will be. You will wonder if you really want to continue. You know you want this intimacy. You NEED this love! You can no longer live with out it. It feels like you will die if you can't have it. But, it is scary. Nothing in the world holds any attraction to you. The church looks shallow and clueless. You no longer belong here!

73

David, too, Faced the Fear of Intimacy

David faced a similar fear. He wanted the Ark of the Covenant in the City of David. The Ark held the presence of God. As they were bringing the Ark home, it began to fall and Uzza reached out and touched the Ark to steady it. He died immediately! NO ONE was to touch the glory of God. (1 Chronicles 13)

David wanted to rejoice in the presence of God, but feared the power of God. So, he decided to take the Ark to the house of Obededom the Gittite. Very quickly, David changed his mind and decided to bring the Ark home. He was so excited about bringing the presence of God home that he publicly sang and danced in his underwear!

David's wife, Michal, disapproved of freedom of expression.

Once the Ark was home in a tabernacle prepared for it, God was worshipped twenty-four hours a day!

The Road Less Traveled

Not only will others be uncomfortable with the fire that consumes our flesh, they will disapprove of our freedom in worship. They will disapprove of our desire not to be part of this world. They will disapprove of the terms of love that we speak concerning our relationship with God. They will be uncomfortable with our intensity. They will be convicted by our "no compromise" attitude. In other words, this can be a lonely journey!

Even after revival breaks out, the walk we are choosing will continue to be lonely. While the crowd is swept by the excitement and power of revival, you will be engrossed in loving the Lord! They will be enthralled with what God is doing. You will be enthralled with God, Himself! They will want to go see what God is doing. You will just want to see God.

CHAPTER TEN

THE COST - PART TWO

MY PERSONAL EXPERIENCE

Now that we have discussed the theology of what it will cost you to enter that deep intimate place with the Lord, we need to get real about it. When God called me to leave my prosperous, anointed ministry in Pittsburgh, He told me that He was going to throw me into the deep water to learn to live by faith again. I said: "OK."

He wanted me to leave the church, which I had pioneered, my work at Cornerstone Television as Board member and on air personality, my radio teaching program, my national speaking engagements, the fame, and financial support. He wanted me to become a nobody in no-place for Him. I said: "OK."

He said that moving ahead would require dying to self. I said: "OK."

He told me I had a choice: I could stay where I was and loose spiritual ground, slip back or backslide, or I could pay the price and move ahead. I said: "OK."

The prophets warned me that the price would be very high if I chose to move ahead. I said: "OK."

How bad could it be? God loved me. He had a plan for me. I was a faith believer. I could handle it.

Walk by Faith

God said that He would not give me a plan. Like the Israelites in the wilderness, I was going to move when he said move, stand when he said stand. He told the Israelites that when they saw the cloud and pillar of fire move, they were to break camp and move. When the cloud did not move, they were to camp until it did move. He said He would tell me day by day if He wanted me to do something. I said: "cool."

We had enough equity in our home in the Pittsburgh area to live off for at least two years. This was going to be piece of cake.

But the house didn't sell. We lost it! And, in anticipation of the sale of our house in Pennsylvania, we had bought our new home in Phoenix on our credit card! We had no source of income, no job, no vision, no Church family to support us. We were literally alone in the desert.

Pray for the Place I Have Sent You

He told me to drive every street in our community of Ahwatukee and pray for the people. He sent me up to a mountaintop to pray over the city. He sent me door to door to do evangelism. But He said nothing about income.

I was a faith believer; if God said He would support me, then He would. So, it was no problem to use the credit card in faith, because God's provision was at hand. It had to be! Because of this presumption, we were very close to forced bankruptcy. Expecting God to deliver and provide at any moment, our debt grew to around $100,000.00. We were in extreme want, and even extremely greater perceived need.

Mail-a-manna

We learned to watch for the "mail-a-manna." It seemed that God used the mailman to deliver unexpected support of varying sizes. On two occasions, when we faced a mountain of debt, checks for $10,000.00 arrived in the mail.

On one occasion, when the mountain of debt was smothering me and the need for IMMEDIATE income was pressing, this man of faith was on the floor cursing God for His unfaithfulness and begging for mercy! I got up from the floor, went to the mailbox and found a check for $10,000.00! On each occasion of big checks from unknown sources, there was just enough money to pay the immediate crisis bills, not enough to get us out of debt or give us a cushion; tithe, bring bills current, nothing left.

I'll do it myself

I "figured" I should do what I knew to do, so I started a church. I had started churches and even taught church planting. Out of Faith Community in Pittsburgh, we had started ten churches in ten years. I KNEW how to build a church.

We grew to sixty people, but could not seem to get a break. We could never find worship leadership or attract new members. Everybody in Ahwatukee seemed to want a church with full programs to offer. But for all of our excuses, there was one truth: "...Except the LORD build the house, they labour in vain that build it:" Psalm 127:1b.

After about three years, God closed the church. Within a month, for a variety of reasons, almost all of my congregation moved out of town! I was left with not much more than a few people who visited occasionally. It was clear that this church was closed!

That is when God said that I was no longer a pastor. Now, He had taken my fame, my income, my perfect credit rating, my support system, my purpose, and my identity! And that was the just the first few years!

Permitted to Counsel

God did permit me to do counseling. This was one of my areas of expertise and I am Board Certified in several different areas. But, that did not meet the ongoing financial needs and didn't touch the debt. Many Christians who promised to pay for counseling didn't. I was "stiffed" for between $5,000.00 and $10,000.00 each year in counseling income!

While this kept me busy, it did not feed my soul or my family. Even though, souls were saved, individuals and families healed, and the bound were set free, I remained oppressed and in need.

It Gets Worse

Times were so bad that I started collecting aluminum cans for recycling! Imagine that: Rev. Dr. James A. Laine, Ph.D., Ph.D., Th.D., D.D., digging around in public garbage cans looking for aluminum cans to sell! You think that could not be God? What about when He fed Elijah with road kill dropped by ravens! (1 Kings 16) Elijah had such a close relationship with God that he was raptured; yet God put him to the test!

Lack of Vision

Not knowing where, when, or what, was EXTREMELY painful! I was used to being very much in control. I always had a plan.

Job's Comforters

People from Pittsburgh spread the news that I was obviously in sin because God had abandoned me. Even though I knew they were wrong, I actually questioned it myself, because nothing I tried to do bore fruit and God was quiet, very quiet. How could this be His will?

Food for the Soul

At one point, God permitted me to become a volunteer chaplain for the Sheriff's Office. I loved it! It fed my soul! I worked patrol and led people to the Lord as I supported the deputies. I remember kneeling on a street corner, in uniform, with a teenage runaway girl. She received the Lord! I remember baptizing a man in his bathtub. He was saved after a suicidal episode where he had held police at bay with a shotgun!

I became the Head Chaplain and recruited and trained others. They gave me my own patrol car! I was honored with high awards for action. Then one day, on the way out to my beat, God said: "This is the last day you will do this! Resign when you go in!" He might as well have ripped my heart out! But, I did what I was told.

ILLNESS!

Two months after God told me to resign the doctor told me I could die at any moment. I had no idea that I was ill! Now I'm being told that I am in a life and death battle! I KNEW that I was not going to die! It had just been a month since God had awakened me and given me vision, for the first time since we arrived. He directed me to write two books and prepare for the coming ministry. I couldn't die!

I prayed, went on a diet, and started walking with God for at least an hour early every day. At first, I begged Him to join me and talk to me on the walks. He would not. He just listened as I prayed.

I repented of my lack of trust, my rebellion and my complaining. I got with the program and asked Him what He was trying to accomplish in me. I pledged to do whatever I needed to do to die to self and grow in Him. I gave it all to Him. Kill me if You want, but restore my love! Restore my first love! Let me, like Paul, say that it is no longer I who live, but Christ who lives in me! Restore my love!!!!

The year after I was healed, my wife became ill. Her life was also in the balance!

Finally, Visible Change!

Within a year after my diagnosis, I was healed. Now I was really hungry for that deep love with Him. I realized that I had been making this trial and my suffering all about me. I realized that it was really all about Him! I needed Him so badly that I felt physical pain! As the poets say, my loins burned with desire for His love. I begged Him!!!! Not for any "thing," I begged Him to let me enter that deep love. I no longer cared about *MY* ministry, or what great thing *I* was going to do for Him, or why this process was taking so long. I came to understand that I was born to praise and love Him. I realized that that was all He wanted from me!

I turned my attention to becoming the best worshipper of God that I could be. That was my ministry and my present call.

Things that used to take my time and attention, no longer had any pull on me. All I wanted was to pray and worship, and tell others how much He loved them! I totally stopped listening to secular radio. I chose worship CDs rather than radio. I looked for music that loved Jesus. I had a new prospective on the Word. " Love", "worship", "desire" now meant totally different things to me. Nothing could keep me from my 4:30 a.m. appointment with Jesus! Now He was demanding that I get up and join Him!

So Much for Vision!

You would think that that was it, but it was not. Right after God gave me the vision for my new ministry, three years ago, He sent a man to me who had the same vision and was directed by God to finance the new ministry. He was in a position to make a great deal of money and God had told him to finance it and let me run it.

We met for three years, waiting on God to do it. We were about a month away from closing the deal that would provide the money when God asked a strange question one morning. He said: "So, how long will you trust Me?" I had no idea what He meant, and given that we were so close to victory, it seemed strange.

Two hours later, I was informed that my friend and partner had died of a heart attack. My friend was gone, and so was the provision for the vision!

God demands it all!

CHAPTER ELEVEN

THE COST - PART THREE

PRACTICAL APPLICATION

Brother Lawrence realized that anything that was not God, kept him from God. Anything that took his attention, took it away from God. These are logical assumptions. Friendship with the world and allowing the cares and pleasures of the world to occupy us are a threat to our spiritual growth. The Word calls us to come out the world, not seek to be friends with the world, fill ourselves with good things, and use our time wisely:

"14 Be ye not unequally yoked together with unbelievers: for what fellowship hath righteousness with unrighteousness? And what communion hath light with darkness? 15 And what concord hath Christ with Belial? Or what part hath he that believeth with an infidel? 16 And what agreement hath the temple of God with idols? For ye are the temple of the living God; as God hath said, I will dwell in them, and walk in them; and I will be their God, and they shall be my people. 17 Therefore come out from among them, and be ye separate, saith the Lord, and touch not the unclean thing; and I will receive you, 18 And will be a Father unto you, and ye shall be my sons and daughters, saith the Lord Almighty. 7:1 Having therefore these promises, dearly beloved, let us cleanse ourselves from all filthiness of the flesh and spirit, perfecting holiness in the fear of God." (2 Corinthians 6:14- 7:1)

"4 Ye adulterers and adulteresses, know ye not that the friendship of the world is enmity with God? whosoever therefore will be a friend of the world is the enemy of God. 5 Do ye think that the scripture saith in vain, The spirit that dwelleth in us lusteth to envy? 6 But he giveth more grace. Wherefore he saith, God resisteth the proud, but giveth grace unto the humble." (James 4:4-6)

"3 For all nations have drunk of the wine of the wrath of her fornication, and the kings of the earth have committed fornication with her, and the merchants of the earth are waxed rich through the abundance of her delicacies. 4 And I heard another voice from heaven, saying, Come out of her, my people, that ye be not partakers of her sins, and that ye receive not of her plagues." (Revelation 18:3-4)

"14 Wherefore he saith, Awake thou that sleepest, and arise from the dead, and Christ shall give thee light. 15 See then that ye walk circumspectly, not as fools, but as wise, 16 Redeeming the time, because the days are evil." (Ephesians 5:14-16)

"And that which fell among thorns are they, which, when they have heard, go forth, and are choked with cares and riches and pleasures of this life, and bring no fruit to perfection." Luke 8:14.

EVERYONE ELSE in the world is going a different way! Everyone else is seeking something different. They share common values and goals. They enjoy the same entertainment and love of pleasure.

YOU ARE DIFFERENT! You have been called out. In the Old Testament, God instructed His people to dress different, cut their hair different, and even to be circumcised that their bodies might be different. He wants us to make the inward changes that will affect the way we think and act. We are not of this world.

GI = GO

When your eye is in the light your whole body is filled with light, when your eye is in the darkness, your whole body is filled with darkness. (Paraphrase Matthew 6:22-23)

"20 And he said, That which cometh out of the man, that defileth the man. 21 For from within, out of the heart of men, proceed evil thoughts, adulteries, fornications, murders, 22

Thefts, covetousness, wickedness, deceit, lasciviousness, an evil eye, blasphemy, pride, foolishness: 23 All these evil things come from within, and defile the man." (Mark 7:20-23)

"45 A good man out of the good treasure of his heart bringeth forth that which is good; and an evil man out of the evil treasure of his heart bringeth forth that which is evil: for of the abundance of the heart his mouth speaketh. 46 And why call ye me, Lord, Lord, and do not the things which I say?" (Luke 6:45-46)

"For as he thinketh in his heart, so is he:" (Proverbs 23:7a)

These last three scriptures exemplify the principle: GI = GO, or GARBAGE IN, GARBAGE OUT. You could say that both the world and the Word teach: "you are what you eat."

Every minute you spend paying attention to something other than the Lord is a minute that distracts you from the Lord. Everything you feed on makes you what you are.

Balance

I have already stated that "balance is the key to life." I know that there are people who lock themselves away and immerse themselves in prayer and the Word and end up going crazy. God Himself calls us to balance. That is seen even in the three commandments He gives us:

Love Him with all our heart, and mind, and soul, and strength.

Love our neighbors as ourselves.

Love one another.

This was the balance we saw in Jesus' life. He spent a great deal of time in prayer. He ministered to the hurting and the unsaved. He spent time fellowshipping with the disciples and his friends.

The Mount of Transfiguration also exemplifies this principle. Immediately following their high time, they came down from the mountain to minister to the needy.

The key is that their meditation was on the Lord, their pleasure was in the Lord, their work served the Lord, and their fellowship was with those who also loved the Lord.

The principle is: "Whatever you do, do it as unto the Lord!"

Desire, not Law

This is not a law or a standard of judgment. It is a heart desire. If you want to participate in the Olympics, you will spend hours in practice and hours in testing your skills in competition. If you want to play an instrument, you will spend hours in practice, study, and performance. If you want an academic degree you will spend years of sacrifice in study, and testing. If you want to have a good marriage you will commit a great deal of time and effort to it. If it is of value to obtain, it will cost you a great deal. If it is your life's desire you will not look at the cost! You will be willing to pay WHATEVER IT TAKES! Most of the time, you will actually enjoy the process. [I remember going to wrestling practice in High School and complaining bitterly about how hard it was. Yet, I never missed a practice!]

"44 Again, the kingdom of heaven is like unto treasure hid in a field; the which when a man hath found, he hideth, and for joy thereof goeth and selleth all that he hath, and buyeth that field. 45 Again, the kingdom of heaven is like unto a merchant man, seeking goodly pearls: 46 Who, when he had found one pearl of great price, went and sold all that he had, and bought it." (Matthew 13:44-46)

Lord show me what you require of me. Show me what I must do to get into You. Teach me how to love You in spirit and in truth. Whatever stands in the way remove it. Show me what is pleasing to You and what is not pleasing to You. Draw me unto You! Take away my desire for anything that is not YOU!

CHAPTER TWELVE

THE COST - PART FOUR

PERSONAL CLEANSING

We have talked about the necessity of confession and repentance. We have talked about the necessity for sanctification. We have seen that God's plan is to transform us into the image of the Son, for us to grow up into the fullness of the measure of the stature of Christ. So how do we do this?

Deception

Some of my students are quite tired of hearing me talk about deception. But, before you can begin personal cleansing, you have to realize that you are deceived about yourself. "Every way of a man is right in his own eyes: but the LORD pondereth the hearts." Proverbs 21:2.

Think of some of the great men of the Bible who were deceived. Abraham. David. Solomon. Judas.

Abraham, who is held up as the example of faith, was deceived into creating Ishmael, the father of all Arab nations!

David, a man after God's own heart, committed adultery and murdered to cover it up.

Solomon, the wisest man who ever lived, married many foreign wives.

Judas believed a lie even though he WALKED with Jesus!

Now, Bride of Christ, tell me how you are sure you are not deceived! The human mind works by deception. Your eye works by reflecting the light off the back of your eyeball. There is a hole in the back of your eyeball where the optic nerve comes in. You are seeing nothing reflected off that hole. You have a hole in the vision of each eye. You don't notice it because your brain compensates or *deceives* you into believing that you are seeing the full picture. Trust me, none of us sees the whole picture!

David permitted the prophet to speak into his life and he was convicted of his deception and sin. After that, he would pray "23 Search me, O God, and know my heart: try me, and know my thoughts: 24 And see if there be any wicked way in me, and lead me in the way everlasting." (Psalm 139:23-24) He allowed a man of God, the Holy Spirit, and the Word to examine him and correct him. He did not trust his own judgment.

We first need to realize that even we can be deceived. Then we need to be open to the brethren to speak into our lives. Even more importantly, we need to ask God to search us and try us all the time. When we are convicted, we need to repent.

Walk in the Spirit

"If we live in the Spirit, let us also walk in the Spirit." (Galatians 5:25) Walking in the Spirit means dealing with the works of the flesh.

"16 This I say then, Walk in the Spirit, and ye shall not fulfil the lust of the flesh. 17 For the flesh lusteth against the Spirit, and the Spirit against the flesh: and these are contrary the one to the other: so that ye cannot do the things that ye would. 18 But if ye be led of the Spirit, ye are not under the law. 19 Now the works of the flesh are manifest, which are these; Adultery, fornication, uncleanness, lasciviousness, 20 Idolatry, witchcraft, hatred, variance, emulations, wrath, strife, seditions, heresies, 21 Envyings, murders, drunkenness, revellings, and such like: of the which I tell you before, as I have also told you in time past, that they which do such things shall not inherit the kingdom of God." (Galatians 5:16-21)

These things need to be put to death. Jesus taught us to get aggressive with these issues. He said if your eye offends you, cut it out! If your hand offends you, cut it off! It is better to go into heaven without and eye or a hand than to go into hell whole. (Matthew 5:29-30)

We need to get aggressive with sin. If we do not, it will keep showing up in our lives. It will continue to steal, kill and destroy. It will certainly keep us from standing on God's holy hill and there is no way we will enjoy consistent intimacy with the Lord.

We confess and stop doing what we were doing. We reckon, consider, account ourselves dead to that sin and alive to Christ. (Romans 6:11)

We take authority over the sin and command it out of our lives. We destroy the logical, reasonable, rational arguments that Satan uses to get us to do what we are not supposed to do. We take captive every thought to the obedience of Christ.

(2 Corinthians 10:4-5) We may need to confess our sins to one another (James 5:16) to be healed and to become accountable. We may need to be anointed with oil, have hands laid on and be prayed for to overcome.

Put on the Things of the Spirit

Remember that the process of life is exchange. We can't just stop doing the wrong things; we need to start doing the right things. We must complete the process of exchange. The things we are to put on are love and its attributes. God is love. If we are going to be transformed into the image of the Son, we need to become loving, with all its attributes.

"22 But the fruit of the Spirit is love, joy, peace, longsuffering, gentleness, goodness, faith, 23 Meekness, temperance: against such there is no law. 24 And they that are Christ's have crucified the flesh with the affections and lusts. 25 If we live in the Spirit, let us also walk in the Spirit." (Galatians 5:22-25)

"4 Charity [love] suffereth long, and is kind; charity [love] envieth not; charity [love] vaunteth not itself, is not puffed up, 5 Doth not behave itself unseemly, seeketh not her own, is not easily provoked, thinketh no evil; 6 Rejoiceth not in iniquity, but rejoiceth in the truth; 7 Beareth all things, believeth all things, hopeth all things, endureth all things." (1 Corinthians 13:4-7)

"1 I beseech you therefore, brethren, by the mercies of God, that ye present your bodies a living sacrifice, holy, acceptable unto God, which is your reasonable service. 2 And be not conformed to this world: but be ye transformed by the renewing of your mind, that ye may prove what is that good, and acceptable, and perfect, will of God." Romans 12:1-2

The more we meditate on the Word of God, the more we go through that transformation, metamorphosis process. Following the meditation process helps. Speaking out loud:

What does this verse command me to do or what does it promise to me?
If I really believed it was true, how would I act?
Do I act like I believe it is true?
If not, what am I going to do about it?
I confess it as my reality.
I ask God to change my life to agree with this word.

God's plan for success [not the American idea of success] is found in Joshua 1:7-9: "7 Only be thou strong and very courageous, that thou mayest observe to do according to all the law, which Moses my servant commanded thee: turn not from it to the right hand or to the left, that thou mayest prosper whithersoever thou goest. 8 This book of the law shall not depart out of thy mouth; but thou shalt meditate therein day and night, that thou mayest observe to do according to all that is written therein: for then thou shalt make thy way prosperous, and then thou shalt have good success. 9 have not I commanded thee? Be strong and of a good courage; be not afraid, neither be thou dismayed: for the LORD thy God is with thee whithersoever thou goest."

God says:

Don't be afraid.

Do what the Word says.

Trust me and obey me.

Speak the Word. [One of the biggest mistakes Christians make is not to speak the Word of God! Speaking God's Word helps us to overcome.]

Meditate on the Word day and night. [That means using a process similar to the above. It does not mean "Pastor I read my three chapters today, I'm a good little Christian."] The Word needs to get into us.

Then He says that if we do these things we will have good success!

Love is the Goal

When you can read 1 Corinthians 13:4-7 aloud and replace the word *love* with the word *I*, and you get through the exercise without laughing or choking, you are beginning to get somewhere.

I am patient [long suffering] and kind. I am not jealous [envious] or boastful. I do not act inappropriately. I do not insist on my own way. I am not irritable or resentful. I do not rejoice when bad things happen to others. I do not rejoice at things that are sinful. I rejoice at the truth.

CHAPTER THIRTEEN

HOW?

The question always comes up, "How do it get to be the Bride? How do I develop this intimacy with Jesus?" Brother Lawrence gave us the simple truth. Religious prayers and formulas don't work. Jesus is not a system. He is not a religion. He is The Living God. He is your Bridegroom. He wants a love relationship with you! The only way to come into that relationship is to court Him. Get to know Him. Make friends with Him. Love Him. Make love to Him. You will have to find your own way to do that. I can, however, tell you a few things that are necessary and a few things that will help.

First – Salvation

Before anything else, you *must* be saved. Eternal life is a free gift of grace received by faith, it is not of works, it is not of your own doing, lest any man should boast. (Ephesians 2:8-9) You must know beyond a shadow of a doubt that you cannot enter into the presence of God as a sinful being. God can't look on sin. "Let us therefore come boldly unto the throne of grace, that we may obtain mercy, and find grace to help in time of need." Hebrews 4:16.

You must be so saved that you know, beyond a shadow of a doubt, that you are going to Heaven when you die; not because of your works, but because Jesus took your sin upon Himself and died in your place. He paid for your sin in full. The last thing He said on the cross was, "It is finished." *Tetelestai* in the Greek. That is a word that was used in Greek commerce. It was written across a person's bill when they paid it off. It is literally translated "paid in full." Your debt, your sin, is paid in full. You didn't pay it, Jesus did. He loved you before you were ever born. He made provision for your sin.

Think of it this way: your electric is about to be turned off because you couldn't pay the bill. Your pastor pays the bill and hands it back to you marked "paid in full." When the power company shows up to shut off your electric, are you going to allow them to? I THINK NOT!

Your bill is paid in full by Jesus. He did this so that He could marry you! Accept it! Stand on it! Be forever thankful for it!

No Condemnation

Brother Lawrence reported that Satan frequently showed up to tell him that he could never stand in God's presence because he was a worthless, no good sinner. He had to accept his salvation by grace and trust himself to believe God's Word.

"1 There *is* therefore now no condemnation to them which are in Christ Jesus, who walk not after the flesh, but after the Spirit. 2 For the law of the Spirit of life in Christ Jesus hath made me free from the law of sin and death. 3 For what the law could not do, in that it was weak through the flesh, God sending his own Son in the likeness of sinful flesh, and for sin, condemned sin in the flesh:" Romans 8:1-43.

Just as Brother Lawrence had to tell the devil that his bill was paid in full and he had a right to come boldly before the throne of grace. So every believer must exert his faith in this area. The Accuser of the Brethren condemns us all. "Look where you have been. Look what you have done. How can you ever believe that God will allow you in?!" Satan has been a liar from the very beginning!

My struggle with his tormenting accusations was extremely painful; yet how simple it was to win the victory! Open your mouth and tell Satan the TRUTH, you have been washed, cleansed, justified and sanctified. (1 Corinthians 6:11) Your sin has been removed from you as far as the east is from the west. (Psalm 103:12) God remembers your sin no more. (Hebrew 8:12)

91

After months of depression over Satan's accusations, God asked me why I was listening to the liar. He spoke those scriptures to me and told me to speak them to Satan the next time he showed up. It worked! It worked for Brother Lawrence as well. It will also work for you.

Lordship

Besides knowing Him as Savior, we must also know Him as Lord. If He is not Lord, then He is not Savior.

"21 Not every one that saith unto me, Lord, Lord, shall enter into the kingdom of heaven; but he that doeth the will of my Father which is in heaven. 21 Many will say to me in that day, Lord, Lord, have we not prophesied in thy name? and in thy name have cast out devils? and in thy name done many wonderful works? 23 And then will I profess unto them, I never knew you: depart from me, ye that work iniquity." Matthew 7:21-23.

Lordship means:

Whatever you want, Lord.
Whenever y ou want it, Lord.
Wherever you want it, Lord.
No matter what it costs me.

"If ye keep my commandments, ye shall abide in my love; even as I have kept my Father's commandments, and abide in his love." John 15:10.

The Baptism of the Holy Spirit

Jesus told the disciples: "16 And I will pray the Father, and he shall give you another Comforter, that he may abide with you forever; 17 Even the Spirit of truth; whom the world cannot receive, because it seeth him not, neither knoweth him: but ye know him; for he dwelleth with you, and shall be in you." John 14:16-17.

If you want intimacy with the Lord, you should be willing to allow Him to fill you with His presence.

"4 And, being assembled together with *them*, commanded them that they should not depart from Jerusalem, but wait for the promise of the Father, which, *saith he,* ye have heard of me. 5 For John truly baptized with water; but ye shall be baptized with the Holy Ghost not many days hence. .... 8 But ye shall receive power, after that the Holy Ghost is come upon you: and ye shall be witnesses unto me both in Jerusalem, and in all Judea, and in Samaria, and unto the uttermost part of the earth." Acts 1:4-5,8.

"1 And when the day of Pentecost was fully come, they were all with one accord in one place. 2 And suddenly there came a sound from heaven as of a rushing mighty wind, and it filled all the house where they were sitting. 3 And there appeared unto them cloven tongues like as of fire, and it sat upon each of them. 4 And they were all filled with the Holy Ghost, and began to speak with other tongues, as the Spirit gave them utterance." Acts 2:1-4.

Tongues

You will find it particularly helpful to use the gift of tongues in your communication with the Lord. When your heart is so full that you cannot express what you are feeling, you can tell Him in the Spirit. When you are too asleep to pray in the understanding, you can wake up praying in the spirit. You can discover a whole new language of love.

"5 I would that ye all spake with tongues...15 What is it then? I will pray with the spirit, and I will pray with the understanding also: I will sing with the spirit, and I will sing with the understanding also...18 I thank my God, I speak with tongues more than ye all:" 1 Corinthians 14:5a, 15, 18a.

The gift of tongues is a free gift, just like everything we receive from the Lord. You can't earn it. None are worthy of it. It is available to any who seek it. Don't let your church-ology hold you back! Allow His heavenly language to bless both of you!

Prayer

Now we are ready to talk about our conversations with The Bridegroom.

Enter into his gates with thanksgiving, *and* into his courts with praise: be thankful unto him, *and* bless his name." Psalm 100:4.

When a husband and wife get together to be intimate, the husband does not want to hear a bunch of complaints, demands, pleadings, or railings. Neither does the Lord. Spend your time glorifying Him, magnifying Him, thanking Him, and loving Him! He knows your needs. He wants you.

We are taught the prayer guide of A.C.T.S., meaning Adoration, Confession, Thanksgiving, and Supplication. Spend most of your time in adoration. Sing love songs to Him. Eventually, you will hear Him singing back to you! Die to self. Make it all about Him. Celebrate Him and your relationship with Him!

As you begin, don't expect Him to always speak to you while you are praying. You may find Him silent during prayer, but vocal later in the day. He may speak to you when you least expect it.

Tithing

I know, you don't want to hear this one! The last part of us to get saved is our wallets. In marriage, many do not trust their spouse with their finances. Their intimacy is doomed. If you love Him as your husband, you must trust Him and allow Him to handle the finances. If you don't, you are in control and your relationship is out of order. Legally and spiritually, everything you have is His. Will you withhold yourself and wonder why you can't get close to Him?

"6 For I am the LORD, I change not; therefore ye sons of Jacob are not consumed. 7 Even from the days of your fathers ye are gone away from mine ordinances, and have not kept them. Return unto me, and I will return unto you, saith the LORD of hosts. But ye said, Wherein shall we return? 8 Will a man rob God? Yet ye have robbed me. But ye say, Wherein have we robbed thee? In tithes and offerings. 9 Ye are cursed with a curse: for ye have robbed me, even this whole nation. 10 Bring ye all the tithes into the storehouse, that there may be meat in mine house, and prove me now herewith, saith the LORD of hosts, if I will not open you the windows of heaven, and pour you out a blessing, that there shall not be room enough to receive it. 11 And I will rebuke the devourer for your sakes, and he shall not destroy the fruits of your ground; neither shall your vine cast her fruit before the time in the field, saith the LORD of hosts. 12 And all nations shall call you blessed: for ye shall be a delightsome land, saith the LORD of hosts." Malachi 3:6-12.

Confession and Repentance

If there is anything outstanding between you and the Lord, don't just expect to march into His presence and share intimacy as if nothing were wrong! Many a husband has had a fight with his wife and then expected her to meet him sexually without ever healing the wound. It does not work that way!

Sin separates. Adam and Eve heard the sound of God walking in the garden and the hid themselves because they knew they had sinned. (Genesis 3:8-9)

Confession takes two forms. We confess our sin, and then we confess our forgiveness. We must complete this process of exchange. Many people just keep confessing the same sins over and over. They never resolve them or accept the Lord's forgiveness.

Forgiveness

"25 And when ye stand praying, forgive, if ye have ought against any: that your Father also which is in heaven may forgive you your trespasses. 26 But if ye do not forgive, neither will your Father which is in heaven forgive your trespasses." Mark 11:25-26.

One of the biggest problems we face as Christians is unforgiveness. Unforgiveness becomes bitterness. Hebrews 12:15 warns us not to allow any root of bitterness to enter in because by it many things are bittered. It bitters our relationship with Jesus and cuts us off from Him.

Forgiveness is an act of our will. Unforgiveness is a disease that kills. We must forgive all, every time! We must not permit unforgiveness to remain in us! The Lord will not embrace us if we come to Him with unforgiveness in our hearts!

"9 After this manner therefore pray ye: Our Father which art in heaven, Hallowed be thy name. 10 Thy kingdom come.

Thy will be done in earth, as it is in heaven. 11 Give us this day our daily bread. 12 *And forgive us our debts, as we forgive our debtors.*

13 And lead us not into temptation, but deliver us from evil: For thine is the kingdom, and the power, and the glory, for ever. Amen. 14 *For if ye forgive men their trespasses, your heavenly Father will also forgive you: 15 But if ye forgive not men their trespasses, neither will your Father forgive your trespasses.*" Matthew 6:9-15.

"23 Therefore is the kingdom of heaven likened unto a certain king, which would take account of his servants. 24 And when he had begun to reckon, one was brought unto him, which owed him ten thousand talents. 25 But forasmuch as he had not to pay, his lord commanded him to be sold, and his wife, and children, and all that he had, and payment to be made. 26 The servant therefore fell down, and worshipped him, saying, Lord, have patience with me, and I will pay thee all. 27 Then the lord of that servant was moved with compassion, and loosed him, and forgave him the debt. 28 But the same servant went out, and found one of his fellowservants, which owed him an hundred pence: and he laid hands on him, and took him by the throat, saying, Pay me that thou owest. 29 And his fellowservant fell down at his feet, and besought him, saying, Have patience with me, and I will pay thee all. 30 And he would not: but went and cast him into prison, till he should pay the debt. 31 So when his fellowservants saw what was done, they were very sorry, and came and told unto their lord all that was done. 32 Then his lord, after that he had called him, said unto him, O thou wicked servant, I forgave thee all that debt, because thou desiredst me: 33 Shouldest not thou also have had compassion on thy fellowservant, even as I had pity on thee? 34 And his lord was wroth, and delivered him to the tormentors, till he should pay all that was due unto him. 35 So likewise shall my heavenly Father do also unto you, if ye from your hearts forgive not every one his brother their trespasses." Matthew 18:23-35.

Who will stand?

Psalm 24

"1 A Psalm of David. The earth is the LORD'S, and the fulness thereof; the world, and they that dwell therein. 2 For he hath founded it upon the seas, and established it upon the floods. 3 Who shall ascend into the hill of the LORD? or who shall stand in his holy place? 4 He that hath clean hands, and a pure heart; who hath not lifted up his soul unto vanity, nor sworn deceitfully. 5 He shall receive the blessing from the LORD, and righteousness from the God of his salvation. 6 This is the generation of them that seek him, that seek thy face, O Jacob. Selah. 7 Lift up your heads, O ye gates; and be ye lift up, ye everlasting doors; and the King of glory shall come in. 8 Who is this King of glory? The LORD strong and mighty, the LORD mighty in battle. 9 Lift up your heads, O ye gates; even lift them up, ye everlasting doors; and the King of glory shall come in. 10 Who is this King of glory? The LORD of hosts, he is the King of glory. Selah.

As we have mentioned, the one who finds favor in the sight of the Lord is the one who is willing to be sanctified. That means we put to death the things of the flesh and put on the things of the Spirit. That means that we clean ourselves up before we present ourselves to the Bridegroom.

When the Israelites met God at the mountain in the wilderness, they sanctified themselves first. Before a bride is presented, she is washed, coiffed, perfumed, and made beautiful.

In a marriage, if your wife finds your torn boxers to be a turn off when you approach her to make love, you don't tell her to live with it! [If you do, you need to repent!] If wearing socks to bed puts her off, you put off the socks! Don't try to convince the Lord that you love Him if you continue to do the things that offend Him.

"And whatsoever we ask, we receive of him, because we keep his commandments, and do those things that are pleasing in his sight." 1 John 3:22.

"Try to learn what is pleasing to the Lord." Ephesians 5:10 RSV.

Worship

Once we have stood on our salvation, and confessed and repented of our sin, then we are truly ready to enter into the two-way communication of worship. This is where some of the deepest lovemaking occurs.

Most traditional *Worship Services* actually have little or nothing to do with *worship*. Even in Pentecostal and Charismatic churches, much of what passes for worship, isn't! Even our worship songs sing about Him, not TO Him. Imagine a husband and wife getting together and the wife saying into the air: "My husband is strong, courageous, and wonderful. He is a great husband."

Your husband is RIGHT THERE!! Worship Him! Talk to Him! Sing to Him!

Expect a two-way communication in worship. Many churches would forbid Him to speak, even if He wanted to. Most don't give Him the opportunity.

Study worship in the Book of Revelation. Study worship in the Tabernacle! Praise! Exalt! Magnify! Honor! And, after you have worshipped Him as God, make love to Him as your Husband!

Word

The Word has to be part of your communication with the Lord. If you want to know Him, look there. If you want to know His will, look there. He will use the Word in communicating with you. He will answer questions, direct, guide, encourage, rebuke.

Fasting

John Wesley, the great evangelist, would not ordain any man who would not fast three times a week! Fasting is not just going without food. Fasting is not for loosing weight. Fasting means giving things up, so that you can spend some quality time with the Lord. The food fast also helps to cleanse the body and put the flesh in subjection to the Spirit.

Don't fast religiously!!! Fast as God directs. Don't fast to get Him to pay attention to you. Fast to open yourself up to Him.

Don't tell anyone except your spouse that you are fasting. Otherwise, it becomes an issue of spiritual pride to let others know how holy you are. The Word also teaches that letting others know what you are doing for the Lord in secret negates the benefit.

Get real!

Who are we kidding? We don't tell God what we are feeling or what we are thinking. We don't tell Him when we are angry with Him! We can't say that; He is God! How foolish are our small minds. He already knows what we are thinking and feeling. Before the word is ever on our tongues, He knows all about it!

A friendship in which we do not share our deep intimate feelings is a shallow friendship. We withhold ourselves.

God wants all of you, the good, the bad, and the ugly. He already knows it all. He wants us to be real with Him. How can He minister to us if we don't talk to Him about the things with which we are really dealing?

He will talk to you about anything. He will love you in spite of everything. That is what real friends do!

Practicing the Presence

I highly recommend that you consider going on a "God Hunt." Begin to practice the presence. Allow the Lord to abide with you in all you do. Make Him a part of everything. Intimacy requires openness, honesty, vulnerability and access. He will walk with you, play with you, work with you, plan with you, dream with you and sleep with you. The more a part of your life He becomes, the more intimate your relationship will be.

Communication is the Basis of Life

Communication is the basis of life. When communication diminishes, sickness sets in. When communication ceases, death sets in. There is a technical definition of death that states that the individual is no longer in communication with his environment. He is not asking questions or getting answers, he is feeling nothing, there is no exchange or communication of air; he is dead.

The quality of our marriage communication will determine the quality and depth of our relationship. In marriage, we communicate spiritually, emotionally and physically. In the spirit, we communicate through prayer. In the soul, we communicate through sharing thoughts and feelings. In the flesh, we communicate through intercourse, which means communication.

The quality of our communication with Jesus will determine the quality of our relationship with Him. We are told to love Him with all of heart, and soul, and mind and strength.

Start with the "God hunt" then move on to create an openness on your part to act as though you REALLY believe that God *is* with you wherever you go!

Singing

"Speaking to yourselves in psalms and hymns and spiritual songs, singing and making melody in your heart to the Lord;" Ephesians 5:19.

Music has a way of getting down into our spirits. As we sing the Word, it gets into us. As Satan's music changes the people who listen to it, so singing God's Word changes us. It will also help you memorize scripture, even if memorization is difficult for you. Psalms are in the Book of Psalms. Hymns are the great music of the Church. Spiritual songs include singing in tongues, Spirit-inspired love songs that bubble up out of your heart, and singing the Word to God.

Thanksgiving

"Giving thanks always for all things unto God and the Father in the name of our Lord Jesus Christ;" Ephesians 5:20.

"In every thing give thanks: for this is the will of God in Christ Jesus concerning you." 1 Thessalonians 5:18.

"4 Enter into his gates with thanksgiving, and into his courts with praise: be thankful unto him, and bless his name. 5 For the

LORD is good; his mercy is everlasting; and his truth endureth to all generations." Psalm 100:4-5.

We are not a thankful people. We look at what we do not have rather than what we do have. We do not appreciate things when they are given to us. We need to become thankful if we are going to prosper in our love relationship with God.

We are not thankful for bad things, but we can be thankful that He is with us through them and will bless us in the midst of them. Since we love Him, we can also be assured of Romans 8:28: "And we know that all things work together for good to them that love God, to them who are the called according to his purpose."

Desire!

There is a spiritual principle that states "If you don't wanna, you ain't gonna!" Desire is the ONLY KEY! **HEAR THIS!** You can study all the principles and programs ever written. You can read biographies and testimonies for your entire life, but if you do not have the desire driving you, you will never find intimacy with God!

In time management, we teach that every human being has been granted twenty-four hours a day: white, black, educated, ignorant, rich, poor, American or African native. You WILL do with that twenty-four hours what you WANT to do with them. This always brings objection. People truly believe that their time is not their own. Every moment of every day is yours! God has made you a steward of the time. The time you believe to be controlled by others is time that you have chosen to give away! If your priorities are what you say they are, then prove it by what you do with your time, talent, energy and money!

When it comes to a love relationship with your wife or husband, it requires time, attention, persistence, sacrifice and work. Your relationship with Jesus is just the same. It will not grow to its highest possibility if you make other things your priority. It will not grow if you give up in frustration. The moment you quit trying is the moment you loose any hope of finding that secret place in the Lord!

The Word says: "9 And I say unto you, Ask, and it shall be given you; seek, and ye shall find; knock, and it shall be opened unto you. 10 For every one that asketh receiveth; and he that seeketh findeth; and to him that knocketh it shall be opened. 11 If a son shall ask bread of any of you that is a father, will he give him a stone? or if he ask a fish, will he for a fish give him a serpent? 12 Or if he shall ask an egg, will he offer him a scorpion? 13 If ye then, being evil, know how to give good gifts unto your children: how much more shall your heavenly Father give the Holy Spirit to them that ask him?" Luke 11:9-13.

In the Greek, the words "ask", "seek", and "knock" are continuing action words. In other words, "Ask and keep on asking, seek and keep on seeking, knock and keep on knocking". In this instant generation, we give up if our affections are not rewarded right away. Look at the Song of Songs! Seeking, finding, missing, longing, begging, loving, missing!!

If a love relationship with Jesus is what you truly desire, you will spend much time in the pursuit and you will longingly press on, even when you efforts appear to be unrewarded.

Make Love to Him!

When I was newly married and young and foolish, I went out and bought a book that told me how to make love to my wife. I did exactly what the book taught. My wife was not pleased! The mistake I made was not asking her to teach me how to love her! We do the same thing with the Lord.

My experience with Jesus is MY experience with Him. He has taught me how He wants ME to make love to Him. I have no clue, beyond the basics, what He wants from you. You may be able to give Him something I can't. For His sake, I hope that is true. How sad it would be, if all He is receiving were what I am giving to Him! He is worthy of so much more than I can provide for Him!!

Please, explore His love for you! Please, explore how He wants you to make love to Him! Please minister to His heart! Please dedicate yourself to Him to become the best lover He has ever had!

CHAPTER FOURTEEN

RELEASE!

A month after the death of my friend, God started talking to me about Keith Green, an intense prophetic singer who died in 1982. God ministered to me about his intensity and his dissatisfaction with the status quo and the secular spirit of the church. He called people to get real, to "get bananas about Jesus." He called people to go and preach the gospel and save the lost. God told me that He was putting Keith's prophetic anointing on me!

Keith had gotten to the point that he felt like he did not belong here. I got that way very quickly. In fact, while listening to an internationally famous worship team, I told the Lord that I had had it. I was ready to go home! I just wanted to be released to go home and love Him! The church has failed, His people have failed and even our best worship has failed! It was all about us. It was NOT about Him! I was totally dissatisfied with everything around me. Nothing satisfied except my personal love-making time with Jesus. I wanted out! I was done!

The next day, I was to meet with my brother in Christ, Pastor Ken Huhn. He was one of the few brothers from Pittsburgh who continued to believe in me and support me. He was coming to Phoenix to see me and to play golf with one of his elders. My intent was to ask Ken to pray for me that I might go to be with Jesus.

God had other plans! That day, right before I met with Ken, a prophet came to me with a word. She told me that the work that God was doing in me was complete. That He was releasing me to the ministry for which He had been preparing me. He said that

He would restore me and would reveal over the coming days and months what I was to do. He, also, praised my wife for her faithfulness. [He said other things, too personal for this book.] Her word left me dazed, wondering, questioning and vulnerable to God. I immediately told my wife what the Lord had said.

That evening when we met with Ken, he told us that God had given him a word for me during their morning worship service. The word was Isaiah 6:

"1 In the year that king Uzziah died I saw also the Lord sitting upon a throne, high and lifted up, and his train filled the temple. 2 Above it stood the seraphims: each one had six wings; with twain he covered his face, and with twain he covered his feet, and with twain he did fly. 3 And one cried unto another, and said, Holy, holy, holy, *is* the LORD of hosts: the whole earth *is* full of his glory. 4 And the posts of the door moved at the voice of him that cried, and the house was filled with smoke.

5 Then said I, Woe *is* me! for I am undone; because I *am* a man of unclean lips, and I dwell in the midst of a people of unclean lips: for mine eyes have seen the King, the LORD of hosts. 6 Then flew one of the seraphims unto me, having a live coal in his hand, *which* he had taken with the tongs from off the altar: 7And he laid *it* upon my mouth, and said, Lo, this hath touched thy lips; and thine iniquity is taken away, and thy sin purged. 8 Also I heard the voice of the Lord, saying, Whom shall I send, and who will go for us? Then said I, Here *am* I; send me.

9And he said, Go...."

Ken had no idea how important that was! First of all, Isaiah 6 had always been important to me personally. Many years ago I had said to the Lord, "Here I am, send me." I also have a plaque that says that on the wall in my office. It had also been important because Isaiah saw the Lord and repented.

Just the day before, our Pastor's fourteen-year-old daughter, Amy, had preached this passage. King Uzziah's death was significant because he was so important to Isaiah. His death was a great loss to Isaiah and to Israel. In the context of that loss, Isaiah SAW the Lord! He was ready to worship, ready to hear and ready to go!

Ken said that God told him that the death of my friend Jim was like the death of King Uzziah to me. He had been extremely important to me! I had been waiting on him to bring the victory. Now it was time to see the Lord, listen, and go!

I now personally understood what Paul meant when he said "For me to live is Christ; for me to die is gain"! (Philippians 1:21)

When I was saved, I cried and laughed for three days! Following the prophetic words of that day I cried and laughed for weeks! God just kept downloading information to me. He even woke me earlier than usual and told me he had things to tell me. One morning He dragged me out of bed exceptionally early. He told me he had something to say. I barely started to worship and broke down in tears. God said: "Shut up and listen to me. It's my turn. I talk, you listen!" He would not permit worship or prayer that day. He just kept speaking!!!

Now the fire burns! Now the intensity begins! Now the message takes form! Now the urgency becomes clear! Now there is reason to live again. He restoreth my soul!

Glory To The King Of Kings! The season in the Body of Christ has changed!

CHAPTER FIFTEEN

THE PROPOSAL

On one occasion when God was demanding my attention, He spoke to me about the way in which I was to do altar calls. I was to speak first to those who considered themselves to be believers. I was to tell them that many of them had entered a faulty marriage covenant with Him. For years I had preached that people who were fornicating before they married and did not repent, had entered into a faulty marriage covenant and they needed to go back and make it right. Now God was saying that many who thought that they were saved had actually entered a faulty covenant with Him.

In this modern world, many forsake the traditional vows "to love, honor, cherish, and obey" because they do not want to submit to their spouses. They also delete "forsaking all others." They delete "for better or worse, for richer or poorer, in sickness and in health." They do this because of the kingdom of self. Most marriage relationships that fail, fail because of self-centeredness and selfishness. This is lust. It is the opposite of love.

In this modern church, many have married the Lord in the same manner. "I will 'love' you as long as you bless, heal, deliver, and give me prosperity! I want, I need, I will do what I think is required to get you to do what I want. I expect you to meet my needs. I will not promise to forsake all others and I will seek after my own. I will not promise to obey, because after all, I have rights, too."

No one with this attitude is going to prosper in their marriage or in their relationship with Jesus. They will never see true love.

If this pierces your heart, you have a faulty covenant and you need to repent and start again!

We have made our salvation about *us*. We have made our theology about *us*. We have made our worship about *us*. We have made our prayers about *us*. We have made our faith about *us*. We do not love God - WE LUST HIM! And lust is never satisfied or fulfilled.

Full Gospel?

We call ourselves Full Gospel Christians. What a joke! We have just picked different parts of the Gospel to call our own. We have rejected what we don't like or what doesn't fit OUR theology. What about suffering? What about dying to self? What about sacrifice? What about martyrdom? What about repentance and forgiving others? What about dying to self? What about the call to go?

When we preach the prosperity message, the people in China, and Africa and all the people in the church in tribulation, laugh at us! Chinese pastors throw out the prosperity literature we smuggle into their country. All they want is the WORD.

For Better or Worse...

There are seasons, for nations, generations, and individual people. "1 To every *thing there is* a season, and a time to every purpose under the heaven: 2 A time to be born, and a time to die; a time to plant, and a time to pluck up *that which is* planted; 3 A time to kill, and a time to heal; a time to break down, and a time to build up; 4 A time to weep, and a time to laugh; a time to mourn, and a time to dance; 5 A time to cast away stones, and a time to gather stones together; a time to embrace, and a time to refrain from embracing; 6 A time to get, and a time to lose; a time to keep, and a time to cast away; 7 A time to rend, and a time to sew; a time to keep silence, and a time to speak; 8 A time to love, and a time to hate; a time of war, and a time of peace." Ecclesiastes 3:1-8.

That is as much of a Biblical truth as "God will meet your needs according to His riches in Glory"! That way we are to say: "for richer or poorer, in sickness and in health, for better or worse"! That is why Paul said: "12 I know both how to be abased, and I know how to abound: every where and in all things I am instructed both to be full and to be hungry, both to abound and to suffer need. 13 I can do all things through Christ which strengtheneth me." Philippians 4:12-13.

God's Example

God said: "Let me show you the beloved of Christ! Look at your wife, Alice Lee. You took her from her beautiful home where she had a ministry of her own. She was respected, honored and provided for. She had nice things.

You told her that God wanted you both to leave it all and become nobodies in the desert. She said, 'wither thou goest.' You brought her into poverty, want, sickness, and disrespect where she needed to work at menial jobs, suffering disrespect, just to keep things going. Her home was in ill repair and her clothes had holes in them. In twelve years, she NEVER ONCE complained! She never once accused or blamed you. She never demanded that you provide for her. She never once asked you to turn from My plan for you. She LOVED you. Prayed for you, and with you. She supported you. She hurt to see you demeaned! As long as she had you and I, she was OK.

That is the Bride of Christ! That is my covenant keeping betrothed! She IS the virtuous woman!"

To the Unsaved

To the unsaved, Jesus is asking you to become His wife. He is inviting you to accept His marriage proposal RIGHT NOW! "6 Seek ye the LORD while he may be found, call ye upon him while he is near: 7 Let the wicked forsake his way, and the unrighteous man his thoughts: and let him return unto the LORD, and he will have mercy upon him; and to our God, for he will abundantly pardon." Isaiah 55:6-7. This is the hour of His visitation!

If you accept His proposal, today is the day of your salvation! But remember, marrying Him means forsaking all others. It means whatever happens from here on out is up to Him.

If you accept His proposal, it means saying: "*Forsaking all others, I covenant to love, honor, cherish and obey you! I take you, as my spiritually wedded husband in sickness and in health, for richer and for poorer, for better or for worse, until death do us join.*"

The Blessing!

Oh, the joy of being married to one who loves you, heart, soul, mind and strength! The INTIMACY! The exhilaration! The joy! The peace! The security! The fulfillment! You were created for this! This is your highest and best use! This is your highest and best opportunity in life. No matter what happens. No matter WHAT! You will be OK because your husband will always be with you. "Be strong and of a good courage; be not afraid, neither be thou dismayed: for the LORD thy God *is* with thee whithersoever thou goest." Joshua 1:9.

Now you know WHO it is all about. Now you know WHAT it is all about. Now you will come to really know Him who knows you!

CHAPTER SIXTEEN

HE COMES!

You have probably heard "the good news and the bad news." "The good news is that Jesus is coming back. The bad news is that He is angry!"

The Lord is coming back to claim His Bride, the Church. He is coming back for one who is prepared for Him, clean, pure, holy, righteous and loving. He is coming back for a bride that burns with passion in the expectation of His arrival!

If He came today, He would find His Bride full of sin, rebellion, hatred, judgment, strife, sexual perversion, adultery, murder, covetousness, addictions and self-centeredness. He would find a bride who is unfaithful because she is not expecting Him. His people would be terrified if He showed up now!

Are you ready? Are you looking forward? Do you fear what His coming will mean to you? Remember, perfect love casts out all fear, because fear has to do with punishment. (1 John 4:18.) If you are not ready, then you need revival.

Revival!

Revival means many things. There are levels of revival. There are kinds of revivals. Real revival changes people's lives and then changes the life of a nation. As a consequence of the revival of the early 1900's, bars were closed, jails were closed, and judges were laid off. It had a tremendous impact on our nation and the world.

The charismatic revival of the 1960's and 70's got people excited, changed some lives, but did not touch our society. That revival was not marked by repentance. It was characterized by excitement over what God was doing. Any REAL revival will be marked by repentance.

Revival can be both corporate and individual. You as a Lover of Jesus need to be revived in holiness, passion and in fervor. Our nation needs to be revived. The Body of Christ needs to be revived. It all starts with repentance. National, international, worldwide revivals all start with individual repentance. The great Welsh revival of the early 1900's began with individual repentance. The cry of the people was "Lord, bend us lower that Jesus might be exalted!" People bowed themselves to the ground and repented of personal and national sin.

"If my people..."

"14 If my people, which are called by my name, shall humble themselves, and pray, and seek my face, and turn from their wicked ways; then will I hear from heaven, and will forgive their sin, and will heal their land. 15 Now mine eyes shall be open, and mine ears attent unto the prayer that is made in this place. 16 For now have I chosen and sanctified this house, that my name may be there for ever: and mine eyes and mine heart shall be there perpetually." 2 Chronicles 7:14-16.

Repentance

We all need to repent for our sin. Sin separates us from God. Sin pollutes our relationship with Him. Sin cuts us off from His blessings. Sin makes us sick and steals, kills and destroys in our lives. But our repentance must go deeper than stopping those behaviors that are offensive to the Lord.

We were created to love the Lord. Creation is all about Him. We have made it about us. We are selfish, self-centered, willful and self-absorbed. We have loved life, leisure, pleasure, people and things, but we have not loved Jesus! Our repentance must be deep and sincere.

If we feel His pain, if we recognize His loneliness, if we see His hurt at our rejection of Him, if we recognize how totally

111

offensive our behavior has been, then, and only then can we really repent!

Husbands and wives tell one another they are sorry all the time. Sometimes it is said with a sharp tone in the voice, sometimes with a total lack of sincerity, sometimes it clearly means that they are sorry they got caught. It is only real when they realize what they have done and the consequence to the one they love.

Change!

The wife says: "I am sick and tired of hearing you say you are sorry and keep on doing the same thing over again!" Well, saint, Jesus is equally tired of hearing you say you are sorry and asking for forgiveness only to repeat the behavior. If you love Him, keep His commandments! (John 15:10).

Repentance means stopping doing what you are doing and replacing it with right behavior. "Let him that stole steal no more: but rather let him labour, working with his hands the thing which is good, that he may have to give to him that needeth." Ephesians 4:28. It is not enough to say you are sorry and ask for forgiveness. Real change indicates that you really love the Lord and care about what He thinks and feels more than you care about your own desires.

Two-faced God

The God who is coming back has two faces. One face is fierce judgment and brings devouring anger. The other face is gentleness, and tenderness, and brings passionate kisses! It is the very same God! You alone will determine which face you see!

Revival is Coming

Real revival is coming. It is the final revival. It is the revival to cleanse and prepare the bride for her Husband. The revival is coming soon. God has been preparing forerunners to announce its coming. He has been stripping people clean and making love to them so that they would be consumed with the love of the Lord!

When we moved to Phoenix in 1988, we believed that revival was at hand. So did many other leaders in the body. But it did not come. So, the church slipped into lethargy and self-indulgence. We no longer wait expectantly for revival.

The week I was being set free and commissioned to speak, the wife of a pastor friend was having a baby. The nurse checked her and exclaimed that she was dilated eight centimeters and ready to deliver. She ran to call a doctor.

When the nurse returned to check again, she exclaimed that she had been mistaken, the expectant mother was only dilated about four centimeters and the baby was not coming yet. They had plenty of time. Again she left the room to tell the doctor not to rush. The pastor's wife demanded that the nurse check again, because she knew that the baby was coming. The nurse was summoned, and checked yet another time. With one glance she yelled and caught the baby as it was coming out!

The next night, a prophetic word went forth:

You have said that the Coming of Christ is delayed and that the revival is delayed as well. You have plenty of time to get ready. Take your ease and satisfy yourselves!

I say to you that the revival is coming NOW! There is no time to wait. There is no time to prepare. The pastors are not ready. The church is not ready. You did not prepare when I told you to. Now those who are ready will catch the new-borns as they flood out into the world. Now the true Bride will be made manifest!

"1 Then shall the kingdom of heaven be likened unto ten virgins, which took their lamps, and went forth to meet the bridegroom. 2 And five of them were wise, and five *were* foolish. 3 They that *were* foolish took their lamps, and took no oil with them: 4 But the wise took oil in their vessels with their lamps. 5 While the bridegroom tarried, they all slumbered and slept. 6 And at midnight there was a cry made, Behold, the bridegroom cometh; go ye out to meet him. 7 Then all those virgins arose, and trimmed their lamps. 8 And the foolish said unto the wise, Give us of your oil; for our lamps are gone out. 9

But the wise answered, saying, *Not so*; lest there be not enough for us and you: but go ye rather to them that sell, and buy for yourselves. 10 And while they went to buy, the bridegroom came; and they that were ready went in with him to the marriage: and the door was shut. 11 Afterward came also the other virgins, saying, Lord, Lord, open to us. 12 But he answered and said, Verily I say unto you, I know you not. 13 Watch therefore, for ye know neither the day nor the hour wherein the Son of man cometh." Matthew 25:1-13.

Behold He Comes!!

I am as the voice of one crying in the desert, "Prepare ye the way of the Lord!" Oh, how He wants to love you! How He desires to draw you to Himself! How He longs for your passion! How He burns to have you love Him! How jealous He is for you! How He wants to bless you!

Can't you hear Him calling? Don't you feel the hunger?

Your very reason for existence is to love Him. You were created to be His Bride. In the hope that you would choose to love Him, He was willing to put up with sin and rejection, He was willing to suffer the indignity of taking on the form of human flesh, He was willing to suffer and die – FOR YOU! For you, the Omnipotent, Eternal, Omnipresent, Almighty God compressed Himself into the form of a human child! Oh, the indignity! The incredible humility! Then he allowed Himself to be tortured and killed, for you! So that you could live! So that you could love Him and be loved by Him!

"6 Who, being in the form of God, thought it not robbery to be equal with God: 7 But made himself of no reputation, and took upon him the form of a servant, and was made in the likeness of men: 8 And being found in fashion as a man, he humbled himself, and became obedient unto death, even the death of the cross. 9 Wherefore God also hath highly exalted him, and given him a name which is above every name: 10 That at the name of Jesus every knee should bow, of *things* in heaven, and *things* in earth, and *things* under the earth; 11 And *that* every tongue should confess that Jesus Christ *is* Lord, to the glory of God the Father." Philippians 2:6-10.

FOR THE LOVE OF GOD

FOR THE LOVE OF GOD! – How can you not see it?! How can you not respond?! How can you just keep going on like it is all about you?! Your Lover awaits! Run to Him! Embrace Him! Cry out to Him! Run to find Him! Find Him quickly, while there is still time!

"6 Seek ye the LORD while he may be found, call ye upon him while he is near: 7 Let the wicked forsake his way, and the unrighteous man his thoughts: and let him return unto the LORD, and he will have mercy upon him; and to our God, for he will abundantly pardon." Isaiah 55:6-7.

MEDITATION ON THE WORD

The scriptures contained here are to whet your appetite. They are to instruct and aid in meditation on getting "into" the Lord. Remember the meditation process is done aloud:

1. What does this Word tell me about my relationship with the Lord?

   Or what does it command me to do?

   Or what does it promise to me?

2. If I truly believed that this was the Word of God and that it was true, how would I act?

3. Do I act like I believe it is true?

   Does my life reflect this reality?

4. If not, what am I going to do about it?

5. I confess it as my reality.

6. I ask God to make a difference in my life because of it.

7. I make a plan to change my life to reflect this truth.

SONG OF SONGS

1:1-17 The song of songs, which is Solomon's. 2 Let him kiss me with the kisses of his mouth: for thy love is better than wine. 3 Because of the savour of thy good ointments thy name is as ointment poured forth, therefore do the virgins love thee. 4 Draw me, we will run after thee: the king hath brought me into his chambers: we will be glad and rejoice in thee, we will remember thy love more than wine: the upright love thee. 5 I am black, but comely, O ye daughters of Jerusalem, as the tents of Kedar, as the curtains of Solomon. 6 Look not upon me, because I am black, because the sun hath looked upon me: my mother's children were angry with me; they made me the keeper of the vineyards; but mine own vineyard have I not kept. 7 Tell me, O thou whom my soul loveth, where thou feedest, where thou makest thy flock to rest at noon: for why should I be as one that turneth aside by the flocks of thy companions? 8 If thou know not, O thou fairest among women, go thy way forth by the footsteps of the flock, and feed thy kids beside the shepherds' tents. 9 I have compared thee, O my love, to a company of horses in Pharaoh's chariots. 10 Thy cheeks are comely with rows of jewels, thy neck with chains of gold. 11 We will make thee borders of gold with studs of silver. 12 While the king sitteth at his table, my spikenard sendeth forth the smell thereof. 13 A bundle of myrrh is my wellbeloved unto me; he shall lie all night betwixt my breasts. 14 My beloved is unto me as a cluster of camphire in the vineyards of Engedi. 15 Behold, thou art fair, my love; behold, thou art fair; thou hast doves' eyes. 16 Behold, thou art fair, my beloved, yea, pleasant: also our bed is green. 17 The beams of our house are cedar, and our rafters of fir.

Chapter 2

2:1-17 I am the rose of Sharon, and the lily of the valleys. 2 As the lily among thorns, so is my love among the daughters. 3 As the apple tree among the trees of the wood, so is my beloved among the sons. I sat down under his shadow with great delight, and his fruit was sweet to my taste. 4 He brought me to the banqueting house, and his banner over me was love. 5 Stay me with flagons, comfort me with apples: for I am sick of love. 6 His left hand is under my head, and his right hand doth embrace me. 7 I charge you, O ye daughters of Jerusalem, by the roes, and by the hinds of the field, that ye stir not up, nor awake my love, till he please. 8 The voice of my beloved! behold, he cometh leaping upon the mountains, skipping upon the hills. 9 My beloved is like a roe or a young hart: behold, he standeth behind our wall, he looketh forth at the windows, showing himself through the lattice. 10 My beloved spake, and said unto me, Rise up, my love, my fair one, and come away. 11 For, lo, the winter is past, the rain is over and gone; 12 The flowers appear on the earth; the time of the singing of birds is come, and the voice of the turtle is heard in our land; 13 The fig tree putteth forth her green figs, and the vines with the tender grape give a good smell. Arise, my love, my fair one, and come away. 14 O my dove, that art in the clefts of the rock, in the secret places of the stairs, let me see thy countenance, let me hear thy voice; for sweet is thy voice, and thy countenance is comely. 15 Take us the foxes, the little foxes, that spoil the vines: for our vines have tender grapes. 16 My beloved is mine, and I am his: he feedeth among the lilies. 17 Until the day break, and the shadows flee away, turn, my beloved, and be thou like a roe or a young hart upon the mountains of Bether.

Chapter 3

3:1-11 By night on my bed I sought him whom my soul loveth: I sought him, but I found him not. 2 I will rise now, and go about the city in the streets, and in the broad ways I will seek him whom my soul loveth: I sought him, but I found him not. 3 The watchmen that go about the city found me: to whom I said, Saw ye him whom my soul loveth? 4 It was but a little that I passed from them, but I found him whom my soul loveth: I held him, and would not let him go, until I had brought him into my mother's house, and into the chamber of her that conceived me. 5 I charge you, O ye daughters of Jerusalem, by the roes, and by the hinds of the field, that ye stir not up, nor awake my love, till he please. 6 Who is this that cometh out of the wilderness like pillars of smoke, perfumed with myrrh and frankincense, with all powders of the merchant? 7 Behold his bed, which is Solomon's; threescore valiant men are about it, of the valiant of Israel. 8 They all hold swords, being expert in war: every man hath his sword upon his thigh because of fear in the night. 9 King Solomon made himself a chariot of the wood of Lebanon. 10 He made the pillars thereof of silver, the bottom thereof of gold, the covering of it of purple, the midst thereof being paved with love, for the daughters of Jerusalem. 11 Go forth, O ye daughters of Zion, and behold king Solomon with the crown wherewith his mother crowned him in the day of his espousals, and in the day of the gladness of his heart.

Chapter 4

4:1-16 Behold, thou art fair, my love; behold, thou art fair; thou hast doves' eyes within thy locks: thy hair is as a flock of goats, that appear from mount Gilead. 2 Thy teeth are like a flock of sheep that are even shorn, which came up from the washing; whereof every one bear twins, and none is barren among them. 3 Thy lips are like a thread of scarlet, and thy speech is comely: thy temples are like a piece of a pomegranate within thy locks. 4 Thy neck is like the tower of David builded for an armoury, whereon there hang a thousand bucklers, all shields of mighty men. 5 Thy two breasts are like two young roes that are twins, which feed among the lilies. 6 Until the day break, and the shadows flee away, I will get me to the mountain of myrrh, and to the hill of frankincense. 7 Thou art all fair, my love; there is no spot in thee. 8 Come with me from Lebanon, my spouse, with me from Lebanon: look from the top of Amana, from the top of Shenir and Hermon, from the lions' dens, from the mountains of the leopards. 9 Thou hast ravished my heart, my sister, my spouse; thou hast ravished my heart with one of thine eyes, with one chain of thy neck. 10 How fair is thy love, my sister, my spouse! how much better is thy love than wine! and the smell of thine ointments than all spices! 11 Thy lips, O my spouse, drop as the honeycomb: honey and milk are under thy tongue; and the smell of thy garments is like the smell of Lebanon. 12 A garden enclosed is my sister, my spouse; a spring shut up, a fountain sealed. 13 Thy plants are an orchard of pomegranates, with pleasant fruits; camphire, with spikenard, 14 Spikenard and saffron; calamus and cinnamon, with all trees of frankincense; myrrh and aloes, with all the chief spices: 15 A fountain of gardens, a well of living waters, and streams from Lebanon. 16 Awake, O north wind; and come, thou south; blow upon my garden, that the spices thereof may flow out. Let my beloved come into his garden, and eat his pleasant fruits.

Chapter 5

5:1-16 I am come into my garden, my sister, my spouse: I have gathered my myrrh with my spice; I have eaten my honeycomb with my honey; I have drunk my wine with my milk: eat, O friends; drink, yea, drink abundantly, O beloved. 2 I sleep, but my heart waketh: it is the voice of my beloved that knocketh, saying, Open to me, my sister, my love, my dove, my undefiled: for my head is filled with dew, and my locks with the drops of the night. 3 I have put off my coat; how shall I put it on? I have washed my feet; how shall I defile them? 4 My beloved put in his hand by the hole of the door, and my bowels were moved for him. 5 I rose up to open to my beloved; and my hands dropped with myrrh, and my fingers with sweet smelling myrrh, upon the handles of the lock. 6 I opened to my beloved; but my beloved had withdrawn himself, and was gone: my soul failed when he spake: I sought him, but I could not find him; I called him, but he gave me no answer. 7 The watchmen that went about the city found me, they smote me, they wounded me; the keepers of the walls took away my veil from me. 8 I charge you, O daughters of Jerusalem, if ye find my beloved, that ye tell him, that I am sick of love. 9 What is thy beloved more than another beloved, O thou fairest among women? what is thy beloved more than another beloved, that thou dost so charge us? 10 My beloved is white and ruddy, the chiefest among ten thousand. 11 His head is as the most fine gold, his locks are bushy, and black as a raven. 12 His eyes are as the eyes of doves by the rivers of waters, washed with milk, and fitly set. 13 His cheeks are as a bed of spices, as sweet flowers: his lips like lilies, dropping sweet smelling myrrh. 14 His hands are as gold rings set with the beryl: his belly is as bright ivory overlaid with sapphires. 15 His legs are as pillars of marble, set upon sockets of fine gold: his countenance is as Lebanon, excellent as the cedars. 16 His mouth is most sweet: yea, he is altogether lovely. This is my beloved, and this is my friend, O daughters of Jerusalem.

Chapter 6

6:1-13 Whither is thy beloved gone, O thou fairest among women? whither is thy beloved turned aside? that we may seek him with thee. 2 My beloved is gone down into his garden, to the beds of spices, to feed in the gardens, and to gather lilies. 3 I am my beloved's, and my beloved is mine: he feedeth among the lilies. 4 Thou art beautiful, O my love, as Tirzah, comely as Jerusalem, terrible as an army with banners. 5 Turn away thine eyes from me, for they have overcome me: thy hair is as a flock of goats that appear from Gilead. 6 Thy teeth are as a flock of sheep which go up from the washing, whereof every one beareth twins, and there is not one barren among them. 7 As a piece of a pomegranate are thy temples within thy locks. 8 There are threescore queens, and fourscore concubines, and virgins without number. 9 My dove, my undefiled is but one; she is the only one of her mother, she is the choice one of her that bare her. The daughters saw her, and blessed her; yea, the queens and the concubines, and they praised her. 10 Who is she that looketh forth as the morning, fair as the moon, clear as the sun, and terrible as an army with banners? 11 I went down into the garden of nuts to see the fruits of the valley, and to see whether the vine flourished, and the pomegranates budded. 12 Or ever I was aware, my soul made me like the chariots of Amminadib. 13 Return, return, O Shulamite; return, return, that we may look upon thee. What will ye see in the Shulamite? As it were the company of two armies.

Chapter 7

7:1-13 How beautiful are thy feet with shoes, O prince's daughter! the joints of thy thighs are like jewels, the work of the hands of a cunning workman. 2 Thy navel is like a round goblet, which wanteth not liquor: thy belly is like an heap of wheat set about with lilies. 3 Thy two breasts are like two young roes that are twins. 4 Thy neck is as a tower of ivory; thine eyes like the fishpools in Heshbon, by the gate of Bathrabbim: thy nose is as the tower of Lebanon which looketh toward Damascus. 5 Thine head upon thee is like Carmel, and the hair of thine head like purple; the king is held in the galleries. 6 How fair and how pleasant art thou, O love, for delights! 7 This thy stature is like to a palm tree, and thy breasts to clusters of grapes. 8 I said, I will go up to the palm tree, I will take hold of the boughs thereof: now also thy breasts shall be as clusters of the vine, and the smell of thy nose like apples; 9 And the roof of thy mouth like the best wine for my beloved, that goeth down sweetly, causing the lips of those that are asleep to speak. 10 I am my beloved's, and his desire is toward me. 11 Come, my beloved, let us go forth into the field; let us lodge in the villages. 12 Let us get up early to the vineyards; let us see if the vine flourish, whether the tender grape appear, and the pomegranates bud forth: there will I give thee my loves. 13 The mandrakes give a smell, and at our gates are all manner of pleasant fruits, new and old, which I have laid up for thee, O my beloved.

Chapter 8

8:1-14 O that thou wert as my brother, that sucked the breasts of my mother! when I should find thee without, I would kiss thee; yea, I should not be despised. 2 I would lead thee, and bring thee into my mother's house, who would instruct me: I would cause thee to drink of spiced wine of the juice of my pomegranate. 3 His left hand should be under my head, and his right hand should embrace me. 4 I charge you, O daughters of Jerusalem, that ye stir not up, nor awake my love, until he please. 5 Who is this that cometh up from the wilderness, leaning upon her beloved? I raised thee up under the apple tree: there thy mother brought thee forth: there she brought thee forth that bare thee. 6 Set me as a seal upon thine heart, as a seal upon thine arm: for love is strong as death; jealousy is cruel as the grave: the coals thereof are coals of fire, which hath a most vehement flame. 7 Many waters cannot quench love, neither can the floods drown it: if a man would give all the substance of his house for love, it would utterly be contemned. 8 We have a little sister, and she hath no breasts: what shall we do for our sister in the day when she shall be spoken for? 9 If she be a wall, we will build upon her a palace of silver: and if she be a door, we will enclose her with boards of cedar. 10 I am a wall, and my breasts like towers: then was I in his eyes as one that found favour. 11 Solomon had a vineyard at Baalhamon; he let out the vineyard unto keepers; every one for the fruit thereof was to bring a thousand pieces of silver. 12 My vineyard, which is mine, is before me: thou, O Solomon, must have a thousand, and those that keep the fruit thereof two hundred. 13 Thou that dwellest in the gardens, the companions hearken to thy voice: cause me to hear it. 14 Make haste, my beloved, and be thou like to a roe or to a young hart upon the mountains of spices.

LOVE
1 Corinthians 13

12:31 But covet earnestly the best gifts: and yet show I unto you a more excellent way.

13:1-13 Though I speak with the tongues of men and of angels, and have not charity [love], I am become as sounding brass, or a tinkling cymbal. 2 And though I have the gift of prophecy, and understand all mysteries, and all knowledge; and though I have all faith, so that I could remove mountains, and have not charity [love], I am nothing. 3 And though I bestow all my goods to feed the poor, and though I give my body to be burned, and have not charity [love], it profiteth me nothing. 4 Charity [love] suffereth long, and is kind; charity [love] envieth not; charity [love] vaunteth not itself, is not puffed up, 5 Doth not behave itself unseemly, seeketh not her own, is not easily provoked, thinketh no evil; 6 Rejoiceth not in iniquity, but rejoiceth in the truth; 7 Beareth all things, believeth all things, hopeth all things, endureth all things. 8 Charity [love] never faileth: but whether there be prophecies, they shall fail; whether there be tongues, they shall cease; whether there be knowledge, it shall vanish away. 9 For we know in part, and we prophesy in part. 10 But when that which is perfect is come, then that which is in part shall be done away. 11 When I was a child, I spake as a child, I understood as a child, I thought as a child: but when I became a man, I put away childish things. 12 For now we see through a glass, darkly; but then face to face: now I know in part; but then shall I know even as also I am known. 13 And now abideth faith, hope, charity [love], these three; but the greatest of these is charity [love].

14:1a Follow after charity [love], and desire spiritual gifts...

Mark 12:29-31, John 13:34-35

29 And Jesus answered him, The first of all the commandments is, Hear, O Israel; The Lord our God is one Lord: 30 And thou shalt love the Lord thy God with all thy heart, and with all thy soul, and with all thy mind, and with all thy strength: this is the first commandment. 31 And the second is like, namely this, Thou shalt love thy neighbour as thyself. There is none other commandment greater than these.

34 A new commandment I give unto you, That ye love one another; as I have loved you, that ye also love one another. 35 By this shall all men know that ye are my disciples, if ye have love one to another.

(Deu 13:3b) ...for the LORD your God proveth you, to know whether ye love the LORD your God with all your heart and with all your soul.

(Deu 30:6) And the LORD thy God will circumcise thine heart, and the heart of thy seed, to love the LORD thy God with all thine heart, and with all thy soul, that thou mayest live.

(Deu 33:3, 12b) Yea, he loved the people; all his saints are in thy hand: and they sat down at thy feet; every one shall receive of thy words....12b The beloved of the LORD shall dwell in safety by him; and the LORD shall cover him all the day long, and he shall dwell between his shoulders.

(Josh 23:11) Take good heed therefore unto yourselves, that ye love the LORD your God.

(Psa 18:1) To the chief Musician, A Psalm of David, the servant of the LORD, who spake unto the LORD the words of this song in the day that the LORD delivered him from the hand of all his enemies, and from the hand of Saul: And he said, I will love thee, O LORD, my strength.

(Psa 31:23) O love the LORD, all ye his saints: for the LORD preserveth the faithful, and plentifully rewardeth the proud doer.

(Psa 37:4) Delight thyself also in the LORD; and he shall give thee the desires of thine heart.

(Psa 42:1-11) To the chief Musician, Maschil, for the sons of Korah. As the hart panteth after the water brooks, so panteth my soul after thee, O God. 2 My soul thirsteth for God, for the living God: when shall I come and appear before God? 3 My tears have been my meat day and night, while they continually say unto me, Where is thy God? 4 When I remember these things, I pour out my soul in me: for I had gone with the multitude, I went with them to the house of God, with the voice of joy and praise, with a multitude that kept holyday. 5 Why art thou cast down, O my soul? and why art thou disquieted in me? hope thou in God: for I shall yet praise him for the help of his countenance. 6 O my God, my soul is cast down within me: therefore will I remember thee from the land of Jordan, and of the Hermonites, from the hill Mizar. 7 Deep calleth unto deep at the noise of thy waterspouts: all thy waves and thy billows are gone over me. 8 Yet the LORD will command his lovingkindness in the daytime, and in the night his song shall be with me, and my prayer unto the God of my life. 9 I will say unto God my rock, Why hast thou forgotten me? why go I mourning because of the oppression of the enemy? 10 As with a sword in my bones, mine enemies reproach me; while they say daily unto me, Where is thy God? 11 Why art thou cast down, O my soul? and why art thou disquieted within me? hope thou in God: for I shall yet praise him, who is the health of my countenance, and my God.

(Psa 45:1-17) To the chief Musician upon Shoshannim, for the sons of Korah, Maschil, A Song of loves. My heart is inditing a good matter: I speak of the things which I have made touching the king: my tongue is the pen of a ready writer. 2 Thou art fairer than the children of men: grace is poured into thy lips: therefore God hath blessed thee for ever. 3 Gird thy sword upon thy thigh, O most mighty, with thy glory and thy majesty. 4 And in thy majesty ride prosperously because of truth and meekness and righteousness; and thy right hand shall teach thee terrible things. 5 Thine arrows are sharp in the heart of the king's enemies; whereby the people fall under thee. 6 Thy throne, O God, is for ever and ever: the sceptre of thy kingdom is a right sceptre. 7 Thou lovest righteousness, and hatest wickedness: therefore God, thy God, hath anointed thee with the oil of gladness above thy fellows. 8 All thy garments smell of myrrh, and aloes, and cassia, out of the ivory palaces, whereby they have made thee glad. 9 Kings' daughters were among thy honourable women: upon thy right hand did stand the queen in gold of Ophir. 10 Hearken, O daughter, and consider, and incline thine ear; forget also thine own people, and thy father's house; 11 So shall the king greatly desire thy beauty: for he is thy Lord; and worship thou him. 12 And the daughter of Tyre shall be there with a gift; even the rich among the people shall entreat thy favour. 13 The king's daughter is all glorious within: her clothing is of wrought gold. 14 She shall be brought unto the king in raiment of needlework: the virgins her companions that follow her shall be brought unto thee. 15 With gladness and rejoicing shall they be brought: they shall enter into the king's palace. 16 Instead of thy fathers shall be thy children, whom thou mayest make princes in all the earth. 17 I will make thy name to be remembered in all generations: therefore shall the people praise thee for ever and ever.

(Psa 63:1) A Psalm of David, when he was in the wilderness of Judah. O God, thou art my God; early will I seek thee: my soul thirsteth for thee, my flesh longeth for thee in a dry and thirsty land, where no water is; 2 To see thy power and thy glory, so as I have seen thee in the sanctuary. 3 Because thy lovingkindness is better than life, my lips shall praise thee. 4 Thus will I bless thee while I live: I will lift up my hands in thy name. 5 My soul shall be satisfied as with marrow and fatness; and my mouth shall praise thee with joyful lips: 6 When I remember thee upon my bed, and meditate on thee in the night watches. 7 Because thou hast been my help, therefore in the shadow of thy wings will I rejoice. 8 My soul followeth hard after thee: thy right hand upholdeth me.

(Psa 73:25-26) Whom have I in heaven but thee? and there is none upon earth that I desire beside thee. 26 My flesh and my heart faileth: but God is the strength of my heart, and my portion for ever.

(Psa 97:10a) Ye that love the LORD, hate evil...

(Psa 116:1-19) I love the LORD, because he hath heard my voice and my supplications. 2 Because he hath inclined his ear unto me, therefore will I call upon him as long as I live. 3 The sorrows of death compassed me, and the pains of hell gat hold upon me: I found trouble and sorrow. 4 Then called I upon the name of the LORD; O LORD, I beseech thee, deliver my soul. 5 Gracious is the LORD, and righteous; yea, our God is merciful. 6 The LORD preserveth the simple: I was brought low, and he helped me. 7 Return unto thy rest, O my soul; for the LORD hath dealt bountifully with thee. 8 For thou hast delivered my soul from death, mine eyes from tears, and my feet from falling. 9 I will walk before the LORD in the land of the living. 10 I believed, therefore have I spoken: I was greatly afflicted: 11 I said in my haste, All men are liars. 12 What shall I render unto the LORD for all his benefits toward me? 13 I will take the cup of salvation, and call upon the name of the LORD. 14 I will pay my vows unto the LORD now in the presence of all his people. 15 Precious in the sight of the LORD is the death of his saints. 16 O LORD, truly I am thy servant; I am thy servant, and the son of thine handmaid: thou hast loosed my bonds. 17 I will offer to thee the sacrifice of thanksgiving, and will call upon the name of the LORD. 18 I will pay my vows unto the LORD now in the presence of all his people, 19 In the courts of the Lord's house, in the midst of thee, O Jerusalem. Praise ye the LORD.

(Prov 8:17) I love them that love me; and those that seek me early shall find me.

(Prov 23:26) My son, give me thine heart, and let thine eyes observe my ways.

(Jer 2:2-3) Go and cry in the ears of Jerusalem, saying, Thus saith the LORD; I remember thee, the kindness of thy youth, the love of thine espousals, when thou wentest after me in the wilderness, in a land that was not sown. 3 Israel was holiness unto the LORD, and the firstfruits of his increase: all that devour him shall offend; evil shall come upon them, saith the LORD.

(Jer 3:8-11) And I saw, when for all the causes whereby backsliding Israel committed adultery I had put her away, and given her a bill of divorce; yet her treacherous sister Judah feared not, but went and played the harlot also. 9 And it came to pass through the lightness of her whoredom, that she defiled the land, and committed adultery with stones and with stocks. 10 And yet for all this her treacherous sister Judah hath not turned unto me with her whole heart, but feignedly, saith the LORD. 11 And the LORD said unto me, The backsliding Israel hath justified herself more than treacherous Judah.

(Jer 5:7-8) How shall I pardon thee for this? thy children have forsaken me, and sworn by them that are no gods: when I had fed them to the full, they then committed adultery, and assembled themselves by troops in the harlots' houses. 8 They were as fed horses in the morning: every one neighed after his neighbour's wife.

(Jer 23:14) I have seen also in the prophets of Jerusalem an horrible thing: they commit adultery, and walk in lies: they strengthen also the hands of evildoers, that none doth return from his wickedness: they are all of them unto me as Sodom, and the inhabitants thereof as Gomorrah.

(Jer 29:23) Because they have committed villany in Israel, and have committed adultery with their neighbours' wives, and have spoken lying words in my name, which I have not commanded them; even I know, and am a witness, saith the LORD.

(Jer 31:3) The LORD hath appeared of old unto me, saying, Yea, I have loved thee with an everlasting love: therefore with lovingkindness have I drawn thee.

(Mal 1:2a) I have loved you, saith the LORD. Yet ye say, Wherein hast thou loved us?

(Mat 10:37) He that loveth father or mother more than me is not worthy of me: and he that loveth son or daughter more than me is not worthy of me.

(John 3:16-17) For God so loved the world, that he gave his only begotten Son, that whosoever believeth in him should not perish, but have everlasting life. 17 For God sent not his Son into the world to condemn the world; but that the world through him might be saved.

(John 8:42) Jesus said unto them, If God were your Father, ye would love me: for I proceeded forth and came from God; neither came I of myself, but he sent me.

(John 14:15,21, 23) If ye love me, keep my commandments....21 He that hath my commandments, and keepeth them, he it is that loveth me: and he that loveth me shall be loved of my Father, and I will love him, and will manifest myself to him. 23 Jesus answered and said unto him, If a man love me, he will keep my words: and my Father will love him, and we will come unto him, and make our abode with him.

(John 15:9) As the Father hath loved me, so have I loved you: continue ye in my love.

(John 16:27) For the Father himself loveth you, because ye have loved me, and have believed that I came out from God.

(John 17:10,23,26) And all mine are thine, and thine are mine; and I am glorified in them....23 I in them, and thou in me, that they may be made perfect in one; and that the world may know that thou hast sent me, and hast loved them, as thou hast loved me....26 And I have declared unto them thy name, and will declare it: that the love where-with thou hast loved me may be in them, and I in them.

(Acts 21:13) Then Paul answered, What mean ye to weep and to break mine heart? for I am ready not to be bound only, but also to die at Jerusalem for the name of the Lord Jesus.

(Rom 8:28,35,37-79) And we know that all things work together for good to them that love God, to them who are the called according to his purpose... 35 Who shall separate us from the love of Christ? shall tribu-lation, or distress, or persecution, or famine, or nakedness, or peril, or sword?...37 Nay, in all these things we are more than conquerors through him that loved us...38 For I am persuaded, that neither death, nor life, nor angels, nor principalities, nor powers, nor things present, nor things to come, 39 Nor height, nor depth, nor any other creature, shall be able to separate us from the love of God, which is in Christ Jesus our Lord.

(1 Cor 8:3) But if any man love God, the same is known of him.

(1 Cor 16:22) If any man love not the Lord Jesus Christ, let him be Anathema Maranatha.

(2 Cor 5:8) We are confident, I say, and willing rather to be absent from the body, and to be present with the Lord.

(Gal 5:6) For in Jesus Christ neither circumcision availeth any thing, nor uncircumcision; but faith which worketh by love.

(Eph 2:4-5) But God, who is rich in mercy, for his great love where-with he loved us, 5 Even when we were dead in sins, hath quickened us together with Christ, (by grace ye are saved;)

(Eph 3:17-19) That Christ may dwell in your hearts by faith; that ye, being rooted and grounded in love, 18 May be able to comprehend with all saints what is the breadth, and length, and depth, and height;

19 And to know the love of Christ, which passeth knowledge, that ye might be filled with all the fulness of God.

(Eph 4:15) But speaking the truth in love, may grow up into him in all things, which is the head, even Christ:

(Eph 6:24) Grace be with all them that love our Lord Jesus Christ in sincerity. Amen.

(Phil 1:9,23) And this I pray, that your love may abound yet more and more in knowledge and in all judgment;...23 For I am in a strait betwixt two, having a desire to depart, and to be with Christ; which is far better:

(Phil 3:7-8) But what things were gain to me, those I counted loss for Christ. 8 Yea doubtless, and I count all things but loss for the excellency of the knowledge of Christ Jesus my Lord: for whom I have suffered the loss of all things, and do count them but dung, that I may win Christ,

(2 Th 3:5) And the Lord direct your hearts into the love of God, and into the patient waiting for Christ.

(2 Tim 1:7) For God hath not given us the spirit of fear; but of power, and of love, and of a sound mind.

(1 John 2:5,15) But whoso keepeth his word, in him verily is the love of God perfected: hereby know we that we are in him...15 Love not the world, neither the things that are in the world. If any man love the world, the love of the Father is not in him.

(1 John 3:1,16) Behold, what manner of love the Father hath bestowed upon us, that we should be called the sons of God: therefore the world knoweth us not, because it knew him not...16 Hereby perceive we the love of God, because he laid down his life for us: and we ought to lay down our lives for the brethren.

(1 John 4:7-21) Beloved, let us love one another: for love is of God; and every one that loveth is born of God, and knoweth God. 8 He that loveth not knoweth not God; for God is love. 9 In this was manifested the love of God toward us, because that God sent his only begotten Son into the world, that we might live through him. 10 Herein is love, not that we loved God, but that he loved us, and sent his Son to be the propitiation for our sins. 11 Beloved, if God so loved us, we ought also to

love one another. 12 No man hath seen God at any time. If we love one another, God dwelleth in us, and his love is perfected in us. 13 Hereby know we that we dwell in him, and he in us, because he hath given us of his Spirit. 14 And we have seen and do testify that the Father sent the Son to be the Saviour of the world. 15 Whosoever shall confess that Jesus is the Son of God, God dwelleth in him, and he in God. 16 And we have known and believed the love that God hath to us. God is love; and he that dwelleth in love dwelleth in God, and God in him. 17 Herein is our love made perfect, that we may have boldness in the day of judgment: because as he is, so are we in this world. 18 There is no fear in love; but perfect love casteth out fear: because fear hath torment. He that feareth is not made perfect in love. 19 We love him, because he first loved us. 20 If a man say, I love God, and hateth his brother, he is a liar: for he that loveth not his brother whom he hath seen, how can he love God whom he hath not seen? 21 And this commandment have we from him, That he who loveth God love his brother also.

(Jude 1:21) Keep yourselves in the love of God, looking for the mercy of our Lord Jesus Christ unto eternal life.

WORSHIP

(Rev 4:8-11) And the four beasts had each of them six wings about him; and they were full of eyes within: and they rest not day and night, saying, Holy, holy, holy, Lord God Almighty, which was, and is, and is to come. 9 And when those beasts give glory and honour and thanks to him that sat on the throne, who liveth for ever and ever, 10 The four and twenty elders fall down before him that sat on the throne, and worship him that liveth for ever and ever, and cast their crowns before the throne, saying, 11 Thou art worthy, O Lord, to receive glory and honour and power: for thou hast created all things, and for thy pleasure they are and were created.

(Rev 5:8-14) And when he had taken the book, the four beasts and four and twenty elders fell down before the Lamb, having every one of them harps, and golden vials full of odours, which are the prayers of saints. 9 And they sung a new song, saying, Thou art worthy to take the book, and to open the seals thereof: for thou wast slain, and hast redeemed us to God by thy blood out of every kindred, and tongue, and people, and nation; 10 And hast made us unto our God kings and priests: and we shall reign on the earth. 11 And I beheld, and I heard the voice of many angels round about the throne and the beasts and the elders: and the number of them was ten thousand times ten thousand, and thousands of thousands;

12 Saying with a loud voice, Worthy is the Lamb that was slain to receive power, and riches, and wisdom, and strength, and honour, and glory, and blessing. 13 And every creature which is in heaven, and on the earth, and under the earth, and such as are in the sea, and all that are in them, heard I saying, Blessing, and honour, and glory, and power, be unto him that sitteth upon the throne, and unto the Lamb for ever and ever. 14 And the four beasts said, Amen. And the four and twenty elders fell down and worshipped him that liveth for ever and ever.

(1 Chr 15:16, 28) And David spake to the chief of the Levites to appoint their brethren to be the singers with instruments of music, psalteries and harps and cymbals, sounding, by lifting up the voice with joy. ...28 Thus all Israel brought up the ark of the covenant of the LORD with shouting, and with sound of the cornet, and with trumpets, and with cymbals, making a noise with psalteries and harps.

(1 Chr 16:7-36) Then on that day David delivered first this psalm to thank the LORD into the hand of Asaph and his brethren. 8 Give thanks unto the LORD, call upon his name, make known his deeds among the people. 9 Sing unto him, sing psalms unto him, talk ye of all his wondrous works. 10 Glory ye in his holy name: let the heart of them rejoice that seek the LORD. 11 Seek the LORD and his strength, seek his face continually. 12 Remember his marvellous works that he hath done, his wonders, and the judgments of his mouth; 13 O ye seed of Israel his servant, ye children of Jacob, his chosen ones. 14 He is the LORD our God; his judgments are in all the earth. 15 Be ye mindful always of his covenant; the word which he commanded to a thousand generations; 16 Even of the covenant which he made with Abraham, and of his oath unto Isaac; 17 And hath confirmed the same to Jacob for a law, and to Israel for an everlasting covenant, 18 Saying, Unto thee will I give the land of Canaan, the lot of your inheritance; 19 When ye were but few, even a few, and strangers in it. 20 And when they went from nation to nation, and from one kingdom to another people; 21 He suffered no man to do them wrong: yea, he reproved kings for their sakes, 22 Saying, Touch not mine anointed, and do my prophets no harm. 23 Sing unto the LORD, all the earth; show forth from day to day his salvation. 24 Declare his glory among the heathen; his marvellous works among all nations. 25 For great is the LORD, and greatly to be praised: he also is to be feared above all gods 26 For all the gods of the people are idols: but the LORD made the heavens. 27 Glory and honour are in his presence; strength and gladness are in his place. 28 Give unto the LORD, ye kindreds of the people, give unto the LORD glory and strength. 29 Give

unto the LORD the glory due unto his name: bring an offering, and come before him: worship the LORD in the beauty of holiness. 30 Fear before him, all the earth: the world also shall be stable, that it be not moved. 31 Let the heavens be glad, and let the earth rejoice: and let men say among the nations, The LORD reigneth. 32 Let the sea roar, and the fulness thereof: let the fields rejoice, and all that is therein. 33 Then shall the trees of the wood sing out at the presence of the LORD, because he cometh to judge the earth. 34 O give thanks unto the LORD; for he is good; for his mercy endureth for ever. 35 And say ye, Save us, O God of our salvation, and gather us together, and deliver us from the heathen, that we may give thanks to thy holy name, and glory in thy praise. 36 Blessed be the LORD God of Israel for ever and ever. And all the people said, Amen, and praised the LORD.

(1 Chr 25:1a, 6-7) Moreover David and the captains of the host separated to the service of the sons of Asaph, and of Heman, and of Jeduthun, who should prophesy with harps, with psalteries, and with cymbals: ... 6 All these were under the hands of their father for song in the house of the LORD, with cymbals, psalteries, and harps, for the service of the house of God, according to the king's order to Asaph, Jeduthun, and Heman. 7 So the number of them, with their brethren that were instructed in the songs of the LORD, even all that were cunning, was two hundred fourscore and eight.

(1 Chr 29:10-13) Wherefore David blessed the LORD before all the congregation: and David said, Blessed be thou, LORD God of Israel our father, for ever and ever. 11 Thine, O LORD, is the greatness, and the power, and the glory, and the victory, and the majesty: for all that is in the heaven and in the earth is thine; thine is the kingdom, O LORD, and thou art exalted as head above all. 12 Both riches and honour come of thee, and thou reignest over all; and in thine hand is power and might; and in thine hand it is to make great, and to give strength unto all. 13 Now therefore, our God, we thank thee, and praise thy glorious name.

(Psa 8:1-4) To the chief Musician upon Gittith, A Psalm of David. O LORD our Lord, how excellent is thy name in all the earth! who hast set thy glory above the heavens. 2 Out of the mouth of babes and sucklings hast thou ordained strength because of thine enemies, that thou mightest still the enemy and the avenger. 3 When I consider thy heavens, the work of thy fingers, the moon and the stars, which thou hast ordained; 4 What is man, that thou art mindful of him? and the son of man, that thou visitest him?

(Psa 9:1-2) To the chief Musician upon Muthlabben, A Psalm of David. I will praise thee, O LORD, with my whole heart; I will show forth all thy marvellous works. 2 I will be glad and rejoice in thee: I will sing praise to thy name, O thou most High.

(Psa 18:1-3) To the chief Musician, A Psalm of David, the servant of the LORD, who spake unto the LORD the words of this song in the day that the LORD delivered him from the hand of all his enemies, and from the hand of Saul: And he said, I will love thee, O LORD, my strength. 2 The LORD is my rock, and my fortress, and my deliverer; my God, my strength, in whom I will trust; my buckler, and the horn of my salvation, and my high tower. 3 I will call upon the LORD, who is worthy to be praised: so shall I be saved from mine enemies.

(Psa 34:1-3) A Psalm of David, when he changed his behaviour before Abimelech; who drove him away, and he departed. I will bless the LORD at all times: his praise shall continually be in my mouth. 2 My soul shall make her boast in the LORD: the humble shall hear thereof, and be glad. 3 O magnify the LORD with me, and let us exalt his name together.

(Psa 47:1-9) To the chief Musician, A Psalm for the sons of Korah. O clap your hands, all ye people; shout unto God with the voice of triumph. 2 For the LORD most high is terrible; he is a great King over all the earth. 3 He shall subdue the people under us, and the nations under our feet. 4 He shall choose our inheritance for us, the excellency of Jacob whom he loved. Selah. 5 God is gone up with a shout, the LORD with the sound of a trumpet. 6 Sing praises to God, sing praises: sing praises unto our King, sing praises. 7 For God is the King of all the earth: sing ye praises with understanding. 8 God reigneth over the heathen: God sitteth upon the throne of his holiness. 9 The princes of the people are gathered together, even the people of the God of Abraham: for the shields of the earth belong unto God: he is greatly exalted.

(Psa 63:1-8) A Psalm of David, when he was in the wilderness of Judah. O God, thou art my God; early will I seek thee: my soul thirsteth for thee, my flesh longeth for thee in a dry and thirsty land, where no water is; 2 To see thy power and thy glory, so as I have seen thee in the sanctuary. 3 Because thy lovingkindness is better than life, my lips shall praise thee. 4 Thus will I bless thee while I live: I will lift up my hands in thy name. 5 My soul shall be satisfied as with marrow and fatness; and my mouth shall praise thee with joyful lips: 6 When I remember thee upon my bed, and meditate on thee in the night watches. 7 Because thou hast been my help, therefore in the shadow of thy wings will I rejoice. 8 My soul followeth hard after thee: thy right hand upholdeth me.

(Psa 66:1-20) To the chief Musician, A Song or Psalm. Make a joyful noise unto God, all ye lands: 2 Sing forth the honour of his name: make his praise glorious. 3 Say unto God, How terrible art thou in thy works! through the greatness of thy power shall thine enemies submit themselves unto thee. 4 All the earth shall worship thee, and shall sing unto thee; they shall sing to thy name. Selah. 5 Come and see the works of God: he is terrible in his doing toward the children of men. 6 He turned the sea into dry land: they went through the flood on foot: there did we rejoice in him. 7 He ruleth by his power for ever; his eyes behold the nations: let not the rebellious exalt themselves. Selah. 8 O bless our God, ye people, and make the voice of his praise to be heard: 9 Which holdeth our soul in life, and suffereth not our feet to be moved. 10 For thou, O God, hast proved us: thou hast tried us, as silver is tried. 11 Thou broughtest us into the net; thou laidst affliction upon our loins. 12 Thou hast caused men to ride over our heads; we went through fire and through water: but thou broughtest us out into a wealthy place. 13 I will go into thy house with burnt offerings: I will pay thee my vows, 14 Which my lips have uttered, and my mouth hath spoken, when I was in trouble. 15 I will offer unto thee burnt sacrifices of fatlings, with the incense of rams; I will offer bullocks with goats. Selah. 16 Come and hear, all ye that fear God, and I will declare what he hath done for my soul. 17 I cried unto him with my mouth, and he was extolled with my tongue. 18 If I regard iniquity in my heart, the Lord will not hear me: 19 But verily God hath heard me; he hath attended to the voice of my prayer. 20 Blessed be God, which hath not turned away my prayer, nor his mercy from me.

(Psa 69:30) I will praise the name of God with a song, and will magnify him with thanksgiving.

(Psa 90:1-4, 13-17) A Prayer of Moses the man of God. LORD, thou hast been our dwelling place in all generations. 2 Before the mountains were brought forth, or ever thou hadst formed the earth and the world, even from everlasting to everlasting, thou art God. 3 Thou turnest man to destruction; and sayest, Return, ye children of men. 4 For a thousand years in thy sight are but as yesterday when it is past, and as a watch in the night. 13 Return, O LORD, how long? and let it repent thee concerning thy servants. 14 O satisfy us early with thy mercy; that we may rejoice and be glad all our days. 15 Make us glad according to the days wherein thou hast afflicted us, and the years wherein we have seen evil. 16 Let thy work appear unto thy servants, and thy glory unto their children. 17 And let the beauty of the LORD our God be upon us: and establish thou the work of our hands upon us; yea, the work of our hands establish thou it.

(Psa 92:1-5) A Psalm or Song for the sabbath day. It is a good thing to give thanks unto the LORD, and to sing praises unto thy name, O most High: 2 To show forth thy lovingkindness in the morning, and thy faithfulness every night, 3 Upon an instrument of ten strings, and upon the psaltery; upon the harp with a solemn sound. 4 For thou, LORD, hast made me glad through thy work: I will triumph in the works of thy hands. 5 O LORD, how great are thy works! and thy thoughts are very deep.

(Psa 95:1-7) O come, let us sing unto the LORD: let us make a joyful noise to the rock of our salvation. 2 Let us come before his presence with thanksgiving, and make a joyful noise unto him with psalms. 3 For the LORD is a great God, and a great King above all gods. 4 In his hand are the deep places of the earth: the strength of the hills is his also. 5 The sea is his, and he made it: and his hands formed the dry land. 6 O come, let us worship and bow down: let us kneel before the LORD our maker. 7 For he is our God; and we are the people of his pasture, and the sheep of his hand. To day if ye will hear his voice!

(Psa 96:1-13) O sing unto the LORD a new song: sing unto the LORD, all the earth. 2 Sing unto the LORD, bless his name; show forth his salvation from day to day. 3 Declare his glory among the heathen, his wonders among all people. 4 For the LORD is great, and greatly to be praised: he is to be feared above all gods. 5 For all the gods of the nations are idols: but the LORD made the heavens. 6 Honour and majesty are before him: strength and beauty are in his sanctuary. 7 Give unto the LORD, O ye kindreds of the people, give unto the LORD glory and strength. 8 Give unto the LORD the glory due unto his name: bring an offering, and come into his courts. 9 O worship the LORD in the beauty of holiness: fear before him, all the earth. 10 Say among the heathen that the LORD reigneth: the world also shall be established that it shall not be moved: he shall judge the people righteously. 11 Let the heavens rejoice, and let the earth be glad; let the sea roar, and the fulness thereof. 12 Let the field be joyful, and all that is therein: then shall all the trees of the wood rejoice 13 Before the LORD: for he cometh, for he cometh to judge the earth: he shall judge the world with righteousness, and the people with his truth.

(Psa 98:1a, 4-7) A Psalm. O sing unto the LORD a new song; for he hath done marvellous things: his right hand, and his holy arm, hath gotten him the victory. 4 Make a joyful noise unto the LORD, all the earth: make a loud noise, and rejoice, and sing praise. 5 Sing unto the LORD with the harp; with the harp, and the voice of a psalm. 6 With trumpets and sound of cornet make a joyful noise before the LORD, the King. 7 Let the sea roar, and the fulness thereof; the world, and they that dwell therein.

(Psa 100:1-5) A Psalm of praise. Make a joyful noise unto the LORD, all ye lands. 2 Serve the LORD with gladness: come before his presence with singing. 3 Know ye that the LORD he is God: it is he that hath made us, and not we ourselves; we are his people, and the sheep of his pasture. 4 Enter into his gates with thanksgiving, and into his courts with praise: be thankful unto him, and bless his name. 5 For the LORD is good; his mercy is everlasting; and his truth endureth to all generations.

(Psa 103:1-2) A Psalm of David. Bless the LORD, O my soul: and all that is within me, bless his holy name. 2 Bless the LORD, O my soul, and forget not all his benefits:

(Psa 105:1-6) O give thanks unto the LORD; call upon his name: make known his deeds among the people. 2 Sing unto him, sing psalms unto him: talk ye of all his wondrous works. 3 Glory ye in his holy name: let the heart of them rejoice that seek the LORD. 4 Seek the LORD, and his strength: seek his face evermore. 5 Remember his marvellous works that he hath done; his wonders, and the judgments of his mouth; 6 O ye seed of Abraham his servant, ye children of Jacob his chosen.

(Psa 108:1-5) A Song or Psalm of David. O God, my heart is fixed; I will sing and give praise, even with my glory. 2 Awake, psaltery and harp: I myself will awake early. 3 I will praise thee, O LORD, among the people: and I will sing praises unto thee among the nations. 4 For thy mercy is great above the heavens: and thy truth reacheth unto the clouds. 5 Be thou exalted, O God, above the heavens: and thy glory above all the earth;

(Psa 113:1-4) Praise ye the LORD. Praise, O ye servants of the LORD, praise the name of the LORD. 2 Blessed be the name of the LORD from this time forth and for evermore. 3 From the rising of the sun unto the going down of the same the Lord's name is to be praised. 4 The LORD is high above all nations, and his glory above the heavens.

(Psa 117:1-2) O Praise the LORD, all ye nations: praise him, all ye people. 2 For his merciful kindness is great toward us: and the truth of the LORD endureth for ever. Praise ye the LORD.

(Psa 135:1-5) Praise ye the LORD. Praise ye the name of the LORD; praise him, O ye servants of the LORD. 2 Ye that stand in the house of the LORD, in the courts of the house of our God, 3 Praise the LORD; for the LORD is good: sing praises unto his name; for it is pleasant. 4 For the LORD hath chosen Jacob unto himself, and Israel for his peculiar treasure. 5 For I know that the LORD is great, and that our Lord is above all gods.

(Psa 146:1-2) Praise ye the LORD. Praise the LORD, O my soul. 2 While I live will I praise the LORD: I will sing praises unto my God while I have any being.

(Psa 148:1-14) Praise ye the LORD. Praise ye the LORD from the heavens: praise him in the heights. 2 Praise ye him, all his angels: praise ye him, all his hosts. 3 Praise ye him, sun and moon: praise him, all ye stars of light. 4 Praise him, ye heavens of heavens, and ye waters that be above the heavens. 5 Let them praise the name of the LORD: for he commanded, and they were created. 6 He hath also stablished them for ever and ever: he hath made a decree which shall not pass. 7 Praise the LORD from the earth, ye dragons, and all deeps: 8 Fire, and hail; snow, and vapours; stormy wind fulfilling his word: 9 Mountains, and all hills; fruitful trees, and all cedars: 10 Beasts, and all cattle; creeping things, and flying fowl: 11 Kings of the earth, and all people; princes, and all judges of the earth: 12 Both young men, and maidens; old men, and children: 13 Let them praise the name of the LORD: for his name alone is excellent; his glory is above the earth and heaven. 14 He also exalteth the horn of his people, the praise of all his saints; even of the children of Israel, a people near unto him. Praise ye the LORD.

(Psa 150:1-6) Praise ye the LORD. Praise God in his sanctuary: praise him in the firmament of his power. 2 Praise him for his mighty acts: praise him according to his excellent greatness. 3 Praise him with the sound of the trumpet: praise him with the psaltery and harp. 4 Praise him with the timbrel and dance: praise him with stringed instruments and organs. 5 Praise him upon the loud cymbals: praise him upon the high sounding cymbals. 6 Let every thing that hath breath praise the LORD. Praise ye the LORD.

(Isa 6:1-9a) In the year that king Uzziah died I saw also the Lord sitting upon a throne, high and lifted up, and his train filled the temple. 2 Above it stood the seraphims: each one had six wings; with twain he covered his face, and with twain he covered his feet, and with twain he did fly. 3 And one cried unto another, and said, Holy, holy, holy, is the LORD of hosts: the whole earth is full of his glory. 4 And the posts of the door moved at the voice of him that cried, and the house was filled with smoke. 5 Then said I, Woe is me! for I am undone; because I am a man of unclean lips, and I dwell in the midst of a people of unclean lips: for mine eyes have seen the King, the LORD of hosts. 6 Then flew one of the seraphims unto me, having a live coal in his hand, which he had taken with the tongs from off the altar: 7 And he laid it upon my mouth, and said, Lo, this hath touched thy lips; and thine iniquity is taken away, and thy sin purged. 8 Also I heard the voice of the Lord, saying, Whom shall I send, and who will go for us? Then said I, Here am I; send me. 9a And he said, Go...

(Isa 42:10-16) Sing unto the LORD a new song, and his praise from the end of the earth, ye that go down to the sea, and all that is therein; the isles, and the inhabitants thereof. 11 Let the wilderness and the cities thereof lift up their voice, the villages that Kedar doth inhabit: let the inhabitants of the rock sing, let them shout from the top of the mountains. 12 Let them give glory unto the LORD, and declare his praise in the islands. 13 The LORD shall go forth as a mighty man, he shall stir up jealousy like a man of war: he shall cry, yea, roar; he shall prevail against his enemies. 14 I have long time holden my peace; I have been still, and refrained myself: now will I cry like a travailing woman; I will destroy and devour at once. 15 I will make waste mountains and hills, and dry up all their herbs; and I will make the rivers islands, and I will dry up the pools. 16 And I will bring the blind by a way that they knew not; I will lead them in paths that they have not known: I will make darkness light before them, and crooked things straight. These things will I do unto them, and not forsake them.

(John 4:21-24) Jesus saith unto her, Woman, believe me, the hour cometh, when ye shall neither in this mountain, nor yet at Jerusalem, worship the Father. 22 Ye worship ye know not what: we know what we worship: for salvation is of the Jews. 23 But the hour cometh, and now is, when the true worshippers shall worship the Father in spirit and in truth: for the Father seeketh such to worship him. 24 God is a Spirit: and they that worship him must worship him in spirit and in truth.

(Rom 12:1) I beseech you therefore, brethren, by the mercies of God, that ye present your bodies a living sacrifice, holy, acceptable unto God, which is your reasonable service.

(Heb 13:15) By him therefore let us offer the sacrifice of praise to God continually, that is, the fruit of our lips giving thanks to his name.

PRACTICE THE PRESENCE

(Gen 48:15) And he blessed Joseph, and said, God, before whom my fathers Abraham and Isaac did walk, the God which fed me all my life long unto this day,....

(Josh 1:7-9) Only be thou strong and very courageous, that thou mayest observe to do according to all the law, which Moses my servant commanded thee: turn not from it to the right hand or to the left, that thou mayest prosper whithersoever thou goest. 8 This book of the law shall not depart out of thy mouth; but thou shalt meditate therein day and night, that thou mayest observe to do according to all that is written therein: for then thou shalt make thy way prosperous, and then thou shalt have good success. 9 Have not I commanded thee? Be strong and of a good courage; be not afraid, neither be thou dismayed: for the LORD thy God is with thee whithersoever thou goest.

(1 Sam 15:22-23) And Samuel said, Hath the LORD as great delight in burnt offerings and sacrifices, as in obeying the voice of the LORD? Behold, to obey is better than sacrifice, and to hearken than the fat of rams. 23 For rebellion is as the sin of witchcraft, and stubbornness is as iniquity and idolatry. Because thou hast rejected the word of the LORD, he hath also rejected thee from being king.

(2 Sam 22:29) For thou art my lamp, O LORD: and the LORD will lighten my darkness.

(Psa 40:1-8) To the chief Musician, A Psalm of David. I waited patiently for the LORD; and he inclined unto me, and heard my cry. 2 He brought me up also out of an horrible pit, out of the miry clay, and set my feet upon a rock, and established my goings. 3 And he hath put a new song in my mouth, even praise unto our God: many shall see it, and fear, and shall trust in the LORD. 4 Blessed is that man that maketh the LORD his trust, and respecteth not the proud, nor such as turn aside to lies. 5 Many, O LORD my God, are thy wonderful works which thou hast done, and thy thoughts which are to us-ward: they cannot be reckoned up in order unto thee: if I would declare and speak of them, they are more than can be numbered. 6 Sacrifice and offering thou didst not desire; mine ears hast thou opened: burnt offering and sin offering hast thou not required. 7 Then said I, Lo, I come: in the volume of the book it is written of me, 8 I delight to do thy will, O my God: yea, thy law is within my heart.

(Psa 42:1-3) To the chief Musician, Maschil, for the sons of Korah. As the hart panteth after the water brooks, so panteth my soul after thee, O God. 2 My soul thirsteth for God, for the living God: when shall I come and appear before God? 3 My tears have been my meat day and night, while they continually say unto me, Where is thy God?

(Psa 46:7) The LORD of hosts is with us; the God of Jacob is our refuge. Selah.

(Psa 63:1-9) A Psalm of David, when he was in the wilderness of Judah. O God, thou art my God; early will I seek thee: my soul thirsteth for thee, my flesh longeth for thee in a dry and thirsty land, where no water is; 2 To see thy power and thy glory, so as I have seen thee in the sanctuary. 3 Because thy lovingkindness is better than life, my lips shall praise thee. 4 Thus will I bless thee while I live: I will lift up my hands in thy name. 5 My soul shall be satisfied as with marrow and fatness; and my mouth shall praise thee with joyful lips: 6 When I remember thee upon my bed, and meditate on thee in the night watches. 7 Because thou hast been my help, therefore in the shadow of thy wings will I rejoice. 8 My soul followeth hard after thee: thy right hand upholdeth me. 9 But those that seek my soul, to destroy it, shall go into the lower parts of the earth.

(Psa 78:31-39) The wrath of God came upon them, and slew the fattest of them, and smote down the chosen men of Israel. 32 For all this they sinned still, and believed not for his wondrous works. 33 Therefore their days did he consume in vanity, and their years in trouble. 34 When he slew them, then they sought him: and they returned and inquired early after God. 35 And they remembered that God was their rock, and the high God their redeemer. 36 Nevertheless they did flatter him with their mouth, and they lied unto him with their tongues. 37 For their heart was not right with him, neither were they stedfast in his covenant. 38 But he, being full of compassion, forgave their iniquity, and destroyed them not: yea, many a time turned he his anger away, and did not stir up all his wrath. 39 For he remembered that they were but flesh; a wind that passeth away, and cometh not again.

(Psa 81:8-11) Hear, O my people, and I will testify unto thee: O Israel, if thou wilt hearken unto me; 9 There shall no strange god be in thee; neither shalt thou worship any strange god. 10 I am the LORD thy

God, which brought thee out of the land of Egypt: open thy mouth wide, and I will fill it. 11 But my people would not hearken to my voice; and Israel would none of me.

(Psa 83:1b) Keep not thou silence, O God: hold not thy peace, and be not still, O God.

(Psa 84:1-12) To the chief Musician upon Gittith, A Psalm for the sons of Korah. How amiable are thy tabernacles, O LORD of hosts! 2 My soul longeth, yea, even fainteth for the courts of the LORD: my heart and my flesh crieth out for the living God. 3 Yea, the sparrow hath found an house, and the swallow a nest for herself, where she may lay her young, even thine altars, O LORD of hosts, my King, and my God. 4 Blessed are they that dwell in thy house: they will be still praising thee. Selah. 5 Blessed is the man whose strength is in thee; in whose heart are the ways of them. 6 Who passing through the valley of Baca make it a well; the rain also filleth the pools. 7 They go from strength to strength, every one of them in Zion appeareth before God. 8 O LORD God of hosts, hear my prayer: give ear, O God of Jacob. Selah. 9 Behold, O God our shield, and look upon the face of thine anointed. 10 For a day in thy courts is better than a thousand. I had rather be a doorkeeper in the house of my God, than to dwell in the tents of wickedness. 11 For the LORD God is a sun and shield: the LORD will give grace and glory: no good thing will he withhold from them that walk uprightly. 12 O LORD of hosts, blessed is the man that trusteth in thee.

(Psa 91:1-10) He that dwelleth in the secret place of the most High shall abide under the shadow of the Almighty. 2 I will say of the LORD, He is my refuge and my fortress: my God; in him will I trust. 3 Surely he shall deliver thee from the snare of the fowler, and from the noisome pestilence. 4 He shall cover thee with his feathers, and under his wings shalt thou trust: his truth shall be thy shield and buckler. 5 Thou shalt not be afraid for the terror by night; nor for the arrow that flieth by day; 6 Nor for the pestilence that walketh in darkness; nor for the destruction that wasteth at noonday. 7 A thousand shall fall at thy side, and ten thousand at thy right hand; but it shall not come nigh thee. 8 Only with thine eyes shalt thou behold and see the reward of the wicked. 9 Because thou hast made the LORD, which is my refuge, even the most High, thy habitation; 10 There shall no evil befall thee, neither shall any plague come nigh thy dwelling.

(Psa 102:1-2) A Prayer of the afflicted, when he is overwhelmed, and poureth out his complaint before the LORD. Hear my prayer, O LORD, and let my cry come unto thee. 2 Hide not thy face from me in the day when I am in trouble; incline thine ear unto me: in the day when I call answer me speedily.

(Psa 119:33-35) HE. Teach me, O LORD, the way of thy statutes; and I shall keep it unto the end. 34 Give me understanding, and I shall keep thy law; yea, I shall observe it with my whole heart. 35 Make me to go in the path of thy commandments; for therein do I delight.

(Psa 130:1-6) A Song of degrees. Out of the depths have I cried unto thee, O LORD. 2 Lord, hear my voice: let thine ears be attentive to the voice of my supplications. 3 If thou, LORD, shouldest mark iniquities, O Lord, who shall stand? 4 But there is forgiveness with thee, that thou mayest be feared. 5 I wait for the LORD, my soul doth wait, and in his word do I hope. 6 My soul waiteth for the Lord more than they that watch for the morning: I say, more than they that watch for the morning.

(Psa 131:1-2) A Song of degrees of David. LORD, my heart is not haughty, nor mine eyes lofty: neither do I exercise myself in great matters, or in things too high for me. 2 Surely I have behaved and quieted myself, as a child that is weaned of his mother: my soul is even as a weaned child.

(Psa 139:1-18, 23-24) To the chief Musician, A Psalm of David. O LORD, thou hast searched me, and known me. 2 Thou knowest my downsitting and mine uprising, thou understandest my thought afar off. 3 Thou compassest my path and my lying down, and art acquainted with all my ways. 4 For there is not a word in my tongue, but, lo, O LORD, thou knowest it altogether. 5 Thou hast beset me behind and before, and laid thine hand upon me. 6 Such knowledge is too wonderful for me; it is high, I cannot attain unto it. 7 Whither shall I go from thy spirit? or whither shall I flee from thy presence? 8 If I ascend up into heaven, thou art there: if I make my bed in hell, behold, thou art there. 9 If I take the wings of the morning, and dwell in the uttermost parts of the sea; 10 Even there shall thy hand lead me, and thy right hand shall hold me. 11 If I say, Surely the darkness shall cover me; even the night shall be light about me. 12 Yea, the darkness hideth not from thee; but the night shineth as the day: the darkness and the light are both alike to thee. 13 For thou hast possessed my reins: thou hast covered me in my mother's womb. 14 I will praise thee; for I am fearfully and wonderfully made: marvellous are thy works; and that my soul knoweth right well. 15 My substance was not hid from thee, when I was made in secret, and curiously wrought in the lowest parts of the earth. 16 Thine eyes did see my substance, yet being unperfect; and in thy book all my members were written, which in continuance were fashioned, when as yet there was none of them. 17 How precious also are thy thoughts unto me, O God! how great is the sum of them! 18 If I should count them, they are more in number than the sand: when I awake, I am still with thee. ...23 Search me, O God, and know my heart: try me, and know my thoughts: 24 And see if there be any wicked way in me, and lead me in the way everlasting.

(Prov 1:22-33) How long, ye simple ones, will ye love simplicity? and the scorners delight in their scorning, and fools hate knowledge? 23 Turn you at my reproof: behold, I will pour out my spirit unto you, I will make known my words unto you. 24 Because I have called, and ye refused; I have stretched out my hand, and no man regarded; 25 But ye have set at nought all my counsel, and would none of my reproof: 26 I also will laugh at your calamity; I will mock when your fear cometh; 27 When your fear cometh as desolation, and your destruction cometh as a whirlwind; when distress and anguish cometh upon you. 28 Then shall they call upon me, but I will not answer; they shall seek me early, but they shall not find me: 29 For that they hated knowledge, and did not choose the fear of the LORD: 30 They would none of my counsel: they despised all my reproof. 31 Therefore shall they eat of the fruit of their own way, and be filled with their own devices. 32 For the turning away of the simple shall slay them, and the prosperity of fools shall destroy them. 33 But whoso hearkeneth unto me shall dwell safely, and shall be quiet from fear of evil.

(Isa 7:14, Mat 1:23) Therefore the Lord himself shall give you a sign; Behold, a virgin shall conceive, and bear a son, and shall call his name Immanuel. (Mat 1:23) Behold, a virgin shall be with child, and shall bring forth a son, and they shall call his name Emmanuel, which being interpreted is, God with us.

(Isa 26:9) With my soul have I desired thee in the night; yea, with my spirit within me will I seek thee early: for when thy judgments are in the earth, the inhabitants of the world will learn righteousness.

(Isa 41:10) Fear thou not; for I am with thee: be not dismayed; for I am thy God: I will strengthen thee; yea, I will help thee; yea, I will uphold thee with the right hand of my righteousness.

(Isa 43:2) When thou passest through the waters, I will be with thee; and through the rivers, they shall not overflow thee: when thou walkest through the fire, thou shalt not be burned; neither shall the flame kindle upon thee.

(Isa 48:15,17) I, even I, have spoken; yea, I have called him: I have brought him, and he shall make his way prosperous...17 Thus saith the LORD, thy Redeemer, the Holy One of Israel; I am the LORD thy God which teacheth thee to profit, which leadeth thee by the way that thou shouldest go.

(Isa 55:8) For my thoughts are not your thoughts, neither are your ways my ways, saith the LORD.

(Jer 7:23) But this thing commanded I them, saying, Obey my voice, and I will be your God, and ye shall be my people: and walk ye in all the ways that I have commanded you, that it may be well unto you.

(Dan 2:28,47) But there is a God in heaven that revealeth secrets, and maketh known to the king Nebuchadnezzar what shall be in the latter days. Thy dream, and the visions of thy head upon thy bed, are these;...47 The king answered unto Daniel, and said, Of a truth it is, that your God is a God of gods, and a Lord of kings, and a revealer of secrets, seeing thou couldest reveal this secret.

(Hosea 5:15-6:1) I will go and return to my place, till they acknowledge their offence, and seek my face: in their affliction they will seek me early. (Hosea 6:1) Come, and let us return unto the LORD: for he hath torn, and he will heal us; he hath smitten, and he will bind us up.

(Amos 3:7) Surely the Lord GOD will do nothing, but he revealeth his secret unto his servants the prophets.

(Micah 4:2) And many nations shall come, and say, Come, and let us go up to the mountain of the LORD, and to the house of the God of Jacob; and he will teach us of his ways, and we will walk in his paths: for the law shall go forth of Zion, and the word of the LORD from Jerusalem.

(Mat 6:33-34) But seek ye first the kingdom of God, and his righteousness; and all these things shall be added unto you. 34 Take therefore no thought for the morrow: for the morrow shall take thought for the things of itself. Sufficient unto the day is the evil thereof.

(Mat 12:38-39) Then certain of the scribes and of the Pharisees answered, saying, Master, we would see a sign from thee. 39 But he answered and said unto them, An evil and adulterous generation seeketh after a sign; and there shall no sign be given to it, but the sign of the prophet Jonas:

(John 5:17, 19-20) But Jesus answered them, My Father worketh hitherto, and I work. 19 Then answered Jesus and said unto them, Verily, verily, I say unto you, The Son can do nothing of himself, but what he seeth the Father do: for what things soever he doeth, these also doeth the Son likewise. 20 For the Father loveth the Son, and showeth him all things that himself doeth: and he will show him greater works than these, that ye may marvel.

(John 10:2-4) But he that entereth in by the door is the shepherd of the sheep. 3 To him the porter openeth; and the sheep hear his voice: and he calleth his own sheep by name, and leadeth them out. 4 And when he putteth forth his own sheep, he goeth before them, and the sheep follow him: for they know his voice.

(John 14:26) But the Comforter, which is the Holy Ghost, whom the Father will send in my name, he shall teach you all things, and bring all things to your remembrance, whatsoever I have said unto you.

(John 15:1-17) I am the true vine, and my Father is the husbandman. 2 Every branch in me that beareth not fruit he taketh away: and every branch that beareth fruit, he purgeth it, that it may bring forth more fruit. 3 Now ye are clean through the word which I have spoken unto you. 4 Abide in me, and I in you. As the branch cannot bear fruit of itself, except it abide in the vine; no more can ye, except ye abide in me. 5 I am the vine, ye are the branches: He that abideth in me, and I in him, the same bringeth forth much fruit: for without me ye can do nothing. 6 If a man abide not in me, he is cast forth as a branch, and is withered; and men gather them, and cast them into the fire, and they are burned. 7 If ye abide in me, and my words abide in you, ye shall ask what ye will, and it shall be done unto you. 8 Herein is my Father glorified, that ye bear much fruit; so shall ye be my disciples. 9 As the Father hath loved me, so have I loved you: continue ye in my love. 10 If ye keep my commandments, ye shall abide in my love; even as I have kept my Father's commandments, and abide in his love. 11 These things have I spoken unto you, that my joy might remain in you, and that your joy might be full. 12 This is my commandment, That ye love one another, as I have loved you. 13 Greater love hath no man than this, that a man lay down his life for his friends. 14 Ye are my friends, if ye do whatsoever I command you. 15 Henceforth I call you not servants; for the servant knoweth not what his lord doeth: but I have called you friends; for all things that I have heard of my Father I have made known unto you. 16 Ye have not chosen me, but I have chosen you, and ordained you, that ye should go and bring forth fruit, and that your fruit should remain: that whatsoever ye shall ask of the Father in my name, he may give it you. 17 These things I command you, that ye love one another.

(John 16:7-14) Nevertheless I tell you the truth; It is expedient for you that I go away: for if I go not away, the Comforter will not come unto you; but if I depart, I will send him unto you. 8 And when he is come, he will reprove the world of sin, and of righteousness, and of judgment: 9 Of sin, because they believe not on me; 10 Of righteousness, because I go to my Father, and ye see me no more; 11 Of judgment, because the prince of this world is judged. 12 I have yet many things to say unto you, but ye cannot bear them now. 13 Howbeit when he, the Spirit of truth, is come, he will guide you into all truth: for he shall not speak of himself; but whatsoever he shall hear, that shall he speak: and he will show you things to come. 14 He shall glorify me: for he shall receive of mine, and shall show it unto you.

(Acts 2:14-18) But Peter, standing up with the eleven, lifted up his voice, and said unto them, Ye men of Judaea, and all ye that dwell at Jerusalem, be this known unto you, and hearken to my words: 15 For these are not drunken, as ye suppose, seeing it is but the third hour of the day. 16 But this is that which was spoken by the prophet Joel; 17 And it shall come to pass in the last days, saith God, I will pour out of my Spirit upon all flesh: and your sons and your daughters shall prophesy, and your young men shall see visions, and your old men shall dream dreams: 18 And on my servants and on my handmaidens I will pour out in those days of my Spirit; and they shall prophesy:

(1 Cor 2:9-14,16) But as it is written, Eye hath not seen, nor ear heard, neither have entered into the heart of man, the things which God hath prepared for them that love him. 10 But God hath revealed them unto us by his Spirit: for the Spirit searcheth all things, yea, the deep things of God. 11 For what man knoweth the things of a man, save the spirit of man which is in him? even so the things of God knoweth no man, but the Spirit of God. 12 Now we have received, not the spirit of the world, but the spirit which is of God; that we might know the things that are freely given to us of God. 13 Which things also we speak, not in the words which man's wisdom teacheth, but which the Holy Ghost teacheth; comparing spiritual things with spiritual. 14 But the natural man receiveth not the things of the Spirit of God: for they are foolishness unto him: neither can he know them, because they are spiritually discerned...16 For who hath known the mind of the Lord, that he may instruct him? But we have the mind of Christ.

(2 Cor 5:7) (For we walk by faith, not by sight:)

(1 Cor 12:1,4-14) Now concerning spiritual gifts, brethren, I would not have you ignorant. 4 Now there are diversities of gifts, but the same Spirit. 5 And there are differences of administrations, but the same Lord. 6 And there are diversities of operations, but it is the same God which worketh all in all. 7 But the manifestation of the Spirit is given to every man to profit withal. 8 For to one is given by the Spirit the word of wisdom; to another the word of knowledge by the same Spirit; 9 To another faith by the same Spirit; to another the gifts of healing by the same Spirit; 10 To another the working of miracles; to another prophecy; to another discerning of spirits; to another divers kinds of tongues; to another the interpretation of tongues: 11 But all these worketh that one and the selfsame Spirit, dividing to every man severally as he will. 12 For as the body is one, and hath many members, and all the members of that one body, being many, are one body: so also is Christ. 13 For by one Spirit are we all baptized into one body, whether we be Jews or Gentiles, whether we be bond or free; and have been all made to drink into one Spirit. 14 For the body is not one member, but many.

(Phil 2:13) For it is God which worketh in you both to will and to do of his good pleasure.

(Phil 3:10-12) That I may know him, and the power of his resurrection, and the fellowship of his sufferings, being made conformable unto his death; 11 If by any means I might attain unto the resurrection of the dead. 12 Not as though I had already attained, either were already perfect: but I follow after, if that I may apprehend that for which also I am apprehended of Christ Jesus.

(Heb 1:1-2) God, who at sundry times and in divers manners spake in time past unto the fathers by the prophets, 2 Hath in these last days spoken unto us by his Son, whom he hath appointed heir of all things, by whom also he made the worlds;
(Heb 11:6) But without faith it is impossible to please him: for he that cometh to God must believe that he is, and that he is a rewarder of them that diligently seek him.

(James 2:20b)… faith without works is dead?

(1 John 2:15-16) Love not the world, neither the things that are in the world. If any man love the world, the love of the Father is not in him. 16 For all that is in the world, the lust of the flesh, and the lust of the eyes, and the pride of life, is not of the Father, but is of the world.

Individual experiences with God:

Noah – Genesis 6-8	Abram – Genesis 12-13
Isaac –Genesis 26:17-25	Jacob – Genesis 28:10-22
Moses – Exodus 17–24	Joshua – Joshua 3-4
Gideon – Judges 6	Samuel – 1 Samuel 3
Saul – Acts 9:1-25	Elisha – 1 Kings 19:15-21
Rich Ruler – Luke 18:18-27	Simon – Acts 8:9-24

PRAYER

(Psa 63:1) A Psalm of David, when he was in the wilderness of Judah. O God, thou art my God; early will I seek thee: my soul thirsteth for thee, my flesh longeth for thee in a dry and thirsty land, where no water is;

(Psa 134:1-2) A Song of degrees. Behold, bless ye the LORD, all ye servants of the LORD, which by night stand in the house of the LORD. 2 Lift up your hands in the sanctuary, and bless the LORD.

(Mat 6:5-18) And when thou prayest, thou shalt not be as the hypocrites are: for they love to pray standing in the synagogues and in the corners of the streets, that they may be seen of men. Verily I say unto you, They have their reward. 6 But thou, when thou prayest, enter into thy closet, and when thou hast shut thy door, pray to thy Father which is in secret; and thy Father which seeth in secret shall reward thee openly. 7 But when ye pray, use not vain repetitions, as the heathen do: for they think that they shall be heard for their much speaking. 8 Be not ye therefore like unto them: for your Father knoweth what things ye have need of, before ye ask him. 9 After this manner therefore pray ye: Our Father which art in heaven, Hallowed be thy name. 10 Thy kingdom come. Thy will be done in earth, as it is in heaven. 11 Give us this day our daily bread. 12 And forgive us our debts, as we forgive our debtors. 13 And lead us not into temptation, but deliver us from evil: For thine is the kingdom, and the power, and the glory, for ever. Amen. 14 For if ye forgive men their trespasses, your heavenly Father will also forgive you: 15 But if ye forgive not men their trespasses, neither will your Father forgive your trespasses. 16 Moreover when ye fast, be not, as the hypocrites, of a sad countenance: for they disfigure their faces, that they may appear unto men to fast. Verily I say unto you, They have their reward. 17 But thou, when thou fastest, anoint thine head, and wash thy face; 18 That thou appear not unto men to fast, but unto thy Father which is in secret: and thy Father, which seeth in secret, shall reward thee openly.

(Mat 9:37-38) Then saith he unto his disciples, The harvest truly is plenteous, but the labourers are few; 38) Pray ye therefore the Lord of the harvest, that he will send forth labourers into his harvest.

(Mat 17:19-21) Then came the disciples to Jesus apart, and said, Why could not we cast him out? 20 And Jesus said unto them, Because of your unbelief: for verily I say unto you, If ye have faith as a grain of mustard seed, ye shall say unto this mountain, Remove hence to yonder place; and it shall remove; and nothing shall be impossible unto you. 21 Howbeit this kind goeth not out but by prayer and fasting.

(Mat 18:19-20) Again I say unto you, That if two of you shall agree on earth as touching any thing that they shall ask, it shall be done for them of my Father which is in heaven. 20 For where two or three are gathered together in my name, there am I in the midst of them.

(Mat 26:37-43) And he took with him Peter and the two sons of Zebedee, and began to be sorrowful and very heavy. 38 Then saith he unto them, My soul is exceeding sorrowful, even unto death: tarry ye here, and watch with me. 39 And he went a little farther, and fell on his face, and prayed, saying, O my Father, if it be possible, let this cup pass from me: nevertheless not as I will, but as thou wilt. 40 And he cometh unto the disciples, and findeth them asleep, and saith unto Peter, What, could ye not watch with me one hour? 41 Watch and pray, that ye enter not into temptation: the spirit indeed is willing, but the flesh is weak. 42 He went away again the second time, and prayed, saying, O my Father, if this cup may not pass away from me, except I drink it, thy will be done. 43 And he came and found them asleep again: for their eyes were heavy.

(Mark 10:51a) And Jesus answered and said unto him, What wilt thou that I should do unto thee?

(Mark 11:22-26) And Jesus answering saith unto them, Have faith in God. 23 For verily I say unto you, That whosoever shall say unto this mountain, Be thou removed, and be thou cast into the sea; and shall not doubt in his heart, but shall believe that those things which he saith shall come to pass; he shall have whatsoever he saith. 24 Therefore I say unto you, What things soever ye desire, when ye pray, believe that ye receive them, and ye shall have them. 25 And when ye stand praying, forgive, if ye have ought against any: that your Father also which is in heaven may forgive you your trespasses. 26 But if ye do not forgive, neither will your Father which is in heaven forgive your trespasses.

(Luke 5:16) And he withdrew himself into the wilderness, and prayed.

(Luke 11:1-13) And it came to pass, that, as he was praying in a certain place, when he ceased, one of his disciples said unto him, Lord, teach us to pray, as John also taught his disciples. 2 And he said unto them, When ye pray, say, Our Father which art in heaven, Hallowed be thy name. Thy kingdom come. Thy will be done, as in heaven, so in earth. 3 Give us day by day our daily bread. 4 And forgive us our sins; for we also forgive every one that is indebted to us. And lead us not into temptation; but deliver us from evil. 5 And he said unto them, Which of you shall have a friend, and shall go unto him at midnight, and say unto him, Friend, lend me three loaves; 6 For a friend of mine in his journey is come to me, and I have nothing to set before him? 7 And he from within shall answer and say, Trouble me not: the door is now shut, and my children are with me in bed; I cannot rise and give thee. 8 I say unto you, Though he will not rise and give him, because he is his friend, yet because of his importunity he will rise and give him as many as he needeth. 9 And I say unto you, Ask, and it shall be given you; seek, and ye shall find; knock, and it shall be opened unto you. 10 For every one that asketh receiveth; and he that seeketh findeth; and to him that knocketh it shall be opened. 11 If a son shall ask bread of any of you that is a father, will he give him a stone? or if he ask a fish, will he for a fish give him a serpent? 12 Or if he shall ask an egg, will he offer him a scorpion? 13 If ye then, being evil, know how to give good gifts unto your children: how much more shall your heavenly Father give the Holy Spirit to them that ask him?

(Luke 18:1-8) And he spake a parable unto them to this end, that men ought always to pray, and not to faint; 2 Saying, There was in a city a judge, which feared not God, neither regarded man: 3 And there was a widow in that city; and she came unto him, saying, Avenge me of mine adversary. 4 And he would not for a while: but afterward he said within himself, Though I fear not God, nor regard man; 5 Yet because this widow troubleth me, I will avenge her, lest by her continual coming she weary me. 6 And the Lord said, Hear what the unjust judge saith. 7 And shall not God avenge his own elect, which cry day and night unto him, though he bear long with them? 8 I tell you that he will avenge them speedily. Nevertheless when the Son of man cometh, shall he find faith on the earth?

(John 14:12-14) Verily, verily, I say unto you, He that believeth on me, the works that I do shall he do also; and greater works than these shall he do; because I go unto my Father. 13 And whatsoever ye shall ask in my name, that will I do, that the Father may be glorified in the Son. 14 If ye shall ask any thing in my name, I will do it.

(John 15:1-17) I am the true vine, and my Father is the husbandman. 2 Every branch in me that beareth not fruit he taketh away: and every branch that beareth fruit, he purgeth it, that it may bring forth more fruit. 3 Now ye are clean through the word which I have spoken unto you. 4 Abide in me, and I in you. As the branch cannot bear fruit of itself, except it abide in the vine; no more can ye, except ye abide in me. 5 I am the vine, ye are the branches: He that abideth in me, and I in him, the same bringeth forth much fruit: for without me ye can do nothing. 6 If a man abide not in me, he is cast forth as a branch, and is withered; and men gather them, and cast them into the fire, and they are burned. 7 If ye abide in me, and my words abide in you, ye shall ask what ye will, and it shall be done unto you. 8 Herein is my Father glorified, that ye bear much fruit; so shall ye be my disciples. 9 As the Father hath loved me, so have I loved you: continue ye in my love. 10 If ye keep my commandments, ye shall abide in my love; even as I have kept my Father's commandments, and abide in his love. 11 These things have I spoken unto you, that my joy might remain in you, and that your joy might be full. 12 This is my commandment, That ye love one another, as I have loved you. 13 Greater love hath no man than this, that a man lay down his life for his friends. 14 Ye are my friends, if ye do whatsoever I command you. 15 Henceforth I call you not servants; for the servant knoweth not what his lord doeth: but I have called you friends; for all things that I have heard of my Father I have made known unto you. 16 Ye have not chosen me, but I have chosen you, and ordained you, that ye should go and bring forth fruit, and that your fruit should remain: that whatsoever ye shall ask of the Father in my name, he may give it you. 17 These things I command you, that ye love one another.

(John 16:23-26) And in that day ye shall ask me nothing. Verily, verily, I say unto you, Whatsoever ye shall ask the Father in my name, he will give it you. 24 Hitherto have ye asked nothing in my name: ask, and ye shall receive, that your joy may be full. 25 These things have I spoken unto you in proverbs: but the time cometh, when I shall no more speak unto you in proverbs, but I shall show you plainly of the Father. 26 At that day ye shall ask in my name: and I say not unto you, that I will pray the Father for you:

(1 Cor 14:14-15) For if I pray in an unknown tongue, my spirit prayeth, but my understanding is unfruitful. 15 What is it then? I will pray with the spirit, and I will pray with the understanding also: I will sing with the spirit, and I will sing with the understanding also.

(Eph 6:18) Praying always with all prayer and supplication in the Spirit, and watching thereunto with all perseverance and supplication for all saints;

(1 Th 5:16-18) Rejoice evermore. 17 Pray without ceasing. 8 In every thing give thanks: for this is the will of God in Christ Jesus concerning you.

(Heb 11:25) Choosing rather to suffer affliction with the people of God, than to enjoy the pleasures of sin for a season;

(James 4:3-10) Ye ask, and receive not, because ye ask amiss, that ye may consume it upon your lusts. 4 Ye adulterers and adulteresses, know ye not that the friendship of the world is enmity with God? whosoever therefore will be a friend of the world is the enemy of God. 5 Do ye think that the scripture saith in vain, The spirit that dwelleth in us lusteth to envy? 6 But he giveth more grace. Wherefore he saith, God resisteth the proud, but giveth grace unto the humble. 7 Submit yourselves therefore to God. Resist the devil, and he will flee from you. 8 Draw nigh to God, and he will draw nigh to you. Cleanse your hands, ye sinners; and purify your hearts, ye double minded. 9 Be afflicted, and mourn, and weep: let your laughter be turned to mourning, and your joy to heaviness. 10 Humble yourselves in the sight of the Lord, and he shall lift you up.

(James 5:14-16) Is any sick among you? let him call for the elders of the church; and let them pray over him, anointing him with oil in the name of the Lord: 15 And the prayer of faith shall save the sick, and the Lord shall raise him up; and if he have committed sins, they shall be forgiven him. 16 Confess your faults one to another, and pray one for another, that ye may be healed. The effectual fervent prayer of a righteous man availeth much.

(1 John 5:14-15) And this is the confidence that we have in him, that, if we ask any thing according to his will, he heareth us: 15 And if we know that he hear us, whatsoever we ask, we know that we have the petitions that we desired of him.

(Jude 1:20-21) But ye, beloved, building up yourselves on your most holy faith, praying in the Holy Ghost, 21 Keep yourselves in the love of God, looking for the mercy of our Lord Jesus Christ unto eternal life.